Test Wizard

Nicole Gerber

Test Wizard

Automatic test generation based on Design by Contract

VDM Verlag Dr. Müller

Copyright © 2007 VDM Verlag Dr. Müller e. K. and licensors
All rights reserved. Saarbrücken 2007
Contact: info@vdm-verlag.de
Cover image: www.purestockx.com
Publisher: VDM Verlag Dr. Müller e. K., Dudweiler Landstr. 125 a, 66123 Saarbrücken, Germany
Produced by: Lightning Source Inc., La Vergne, Tennessee/USA
              Lightning Source UK Ltd., Milton Keynes, UK

Copyright © 2007 VDM Verlag Dr. Müller e. K. und Lizenzgeber
Alle Rechte vorbehalten. Saarbrücken 2007
Kontakt: info@vdm-verlag.de
Coverbild: www.purestockx.com
Verlag: VDM Verlag Dr. Müller e. K., Dudweiler Landstr. 125 a, 66123 Saarbrücken, Deutschland
Herstellung: Lightning Source Inc., La Vergne, Tennessee/USA
              Lightning Source UK Ltd., Milton Keynes, UK

ISBN: 978-3-8364-1702-0

ACKNOWLEDGEMENTS

First of all I want to thank Karine Arnout for her supervision, her scientific support and her very helpful comments and reviews on this master thesis and Prof. Dr. Bertrand Meyer who made this master thesis possible.

Further I want to thank Xavier Rousselot for his ideas and support concerning the design and implementation of the tool.

I thank also Eric Bezault for his support with the tool *Gobo Eiffel Lint*.

Finally, I am deeply grateful to my parents for their support in every respect.

ABSTRACT

The project is based on the benefits of Design by Contract on testing. If contracts - preconditions, postconditions, class invariants - are systematically associated with classes, they provide an invaluable source of information for producing systematic tests, directly based on the software's expressly intended semantics.

The goal of this project was to develop a tool called *Test Wizard,* which generates test cases automatically from contract-equipped classes. The *Test Wizard* should serve as a workbench to try out different testing strategies.

TABLE OF CONTENTS

LIST OF TABLES

LIST OF FIGURES

1 INTRODUCTION

Testing that a program satisfies its requirements is necessary to prove to the final consumer that the product works. However, testing is often regarded as an expensive and non-rewarding activity. Most companies just produce "good enough" software and ship products that still contain known bugs. (These bugs are often expensive to correct and appear rarely.)

Software products are becoming more complex, interconnecting more and more intricate technologies across multiple operating environments. The size of software products is no longer measured in terms of thousands of lines of code, but millions of lines of code. This increasing complexity of many software products along with a decreasing average market life expectancy has heightened concerns about software quality. The purpose of software engineering is to build high quality software, hence the importance of testing. Testing is a crucial part of software engineering. The cost of testing can range from 50 to 75 percent of the software development budget [13].

Software non-performance and failure are expensive. The media are full of reports of the catastrophic impact of software failures. No business wants an outrage to make the front page of the morning newspaper. Because the cost of testing and verification can exceed the cost of design and programming, the methodologies, techniques, and tools used for testing are key to efficient development of high quality software. According to the NIST report on software testing, the worldwide market for software testing tools was $931 million in 1999 and is projected to grow over $2.6 billion by 2004. Reuse is the key attribute in component-based software engineering. Robert Binder asserts that: *"Components offered for reuse should be highly reliable; ..."* [1], therefore testing gains even more importance.

Reducing the cost of software development and as a part of it reducing the cost of testing and improving software quality are important objectives of software engineering.

The project is based on the benefits of Design by Contract in testing ([6][9][11]). The information given by contracts like preconditions, postconditions and class invariants is highly relevant for testing. The contracts make it possible to produce systematic tests by using only the semantics of software.

If contracts - preconditions, postconditions, class invariants - are systematically associated with classes, they provide an invaluable source of information for producing systematic tests, directly based on the software's expressly intended semantics.

The goal of this project was to develop a tool called *Test Wizard*, which generates test cases automatically from contract-equipped classes [1]. Besides, the goal of the *Test Wizard* was to serve as a workbench to try out different testing strategies.

1

2 PROJECT PLAN

2.1 PROJECT DESCRIPTION

The project description contains the objectives and priorities before starting the project and do not reflect what was actually done. Not everything was realized like described in the project description. Chapter 3 informs about the differences between the actual work and the project plan. This project description is a long-term picture of what a final version of the *Test Wizard* should look like.

2.1.1 SCOPE OF THE WORK

Contracts are a solid information basis to generate black-box test cases automatically. The *Test Wizard* takes an Eiffel library as input and generates test cases using the contract information (see Figure 1 Architecture of the Test Wizard [1]). The test bed I used was the Eiffel library for fundamental structures and algorithms: EiffelBase ([12][8]). The library specification, which is expressed by assertions, is the key to generate black-box test cases automatically. The *Test Wizard* follows a five-step process:

1. **Gathering system information:**
   The Eiffel analyzer parses the library EiffelBase provided as input to retrieve the system information. The system information contains in particular the list of clusters, classes and features in the library.

2. **Defining the test scenarios:**
   Then the tool gathers user information to define the test scenarios. It involves two parts: the information handler and the test scenario handler. The information handler receives the system information and enables the user to choose the following test criteria:

   o Scope of the test:
     The user can select a cluster to be tested (which means all classes of the cluster are tested). The user can also make a more fine-grained selection and choose some classes only, or even just a few features.

   o Exhaustiveness:
     The tool enables changing the number of calls to be performed at several levels: globally, per cluster, per class, and per feature. Moreover the user can control if a feature is tested in descendants.

- Context:
  The tool lets the user decide how classes will be instantiated.
  Predefined bounds are used for common types, such as basic types, besides the user can define bounds for every type.
  The user can also select which creation procedure the tool uses to instantiate classes, overriding the default procedure the tool would choose. Furthermore the user can give the level of randomness of targets and parameters which fixes the number of variants to be created.

- Tolerance:
  The user can define, if a test has passed or not in the case that a rescued exception occurred during a test execution.
  By default, all assertions are checked on the tested features. Nevertheless, the tool also allows partial checking of the assertions. The user can enable or disable the checking of preconditions, postconditions, class invariants, loop invariants and variants, and check instruction to adjust his needs.

- Testing order:
  The user can choose between performing tests on one feature at a time, performing tests on one class at a time or testing as many features as possible (which means calling all requested features once before performing further calls, which is the default policy).

The information handler generates a first test scenario from these user-defined parameters and passes it to the test handler. The test handler outputs the generated scenario and gives the user the opportunity to modify it before the executable gets created. The test handler enables the user to modify:

- Call orderings
- List of calls
- Arguments of the actual calls

3. **Generating a test executable:**
   The code generator generates Eiffel code corresponding to the defined test scenario and calls the Eiffel compiler, which builds the actual test executable. The test executable, which is launched automatically, contains the necessary code to create the context (the pool of test objects). Once the context handler has established the order and means to instantiate the needed classes, the context generator actually generates the objects, and calls modifiers randomly on those objects to build the context. Then the call simulator performs the required calls.

4. **Storing results into a database:**
   Running the test executable and storing the results into a database to handle regression testing.

4

5. Outputting test results:
Displaying the results to the user. The results are classified into four categories:
- o Passed
- o Could not be tested
- o No call was valid
- o Failed

The test result handler provides the user with result information in the following formats:
- o A graphical representation
- o XML files
- o Files using Gobo Eiffel Test format [4]

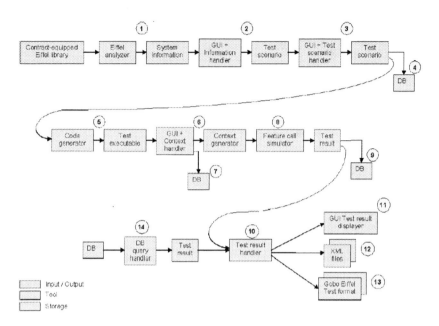

Figure 1 Architecture of the *Test Wizard* [1]

(1) Gather system information.
(2) Display system information to the user and gather user information.
(3) Build the test scenario from the criteria selected by the user.
(4) Store the test scenario into a database (for regression testing).
(5) Generate a test executable corresponding to the test scenario.
(6) Run the executable: it creates a pool of objects (the "Context") possibly helped by the user.
(7) Store the order of class instantiations (for regression testing).
(8) The executable performs feature calls on the pool of instantiated objects.
(9) Store the test results into a database.
(10) Output the results to the users.
(11) Display the results graphically with diagrams.
(12) Generate XML files corresponding to the test results.
(13) Generate files using the Gobo Eiffel Test format.
(14) Query the database and retrieve test results to be passed to the test result handler.

6

2.1.2 INTENDED RESULTS

Implementation:

Eiffel analyzer: The Eiffel analyzer uses the tool *Gobo Eiffel Lint* (*gelint*) ([2][3]) to have access to the system information required by the information handler and makes the required system information available to the information handler.

Information handler: The information handler interacts with a GUI where the user can create a test scenario by feeding test parameters. (The current implementation done during this project does not include any GUI development . This is the long-term picture of the *Test Wizard.*)

Test scenario handler: The test scenario handler also interacts with a GUI where the user can adapt the generated test scenario. (This is again the long-term picture of the *Test Wizard.*)

Code generator: The code generator generates Eiffel code corresponding to the defined test scenario and calls the Eiffel compiler, which builds the actual test executable.

Context handler: The context handler establishes the order and means to instantiate the needed classes.

Context generator: The context generator actually generates the objects, and calls modifiers randomly on those objects to build the context.

Call simulator: The call simulator wraps all calls in a rescue block to handle five possible cases: no exception, exception raised and caught, precondition violation, other assertion violation and other exception.

Test result handler: The test result handler provides the result in three different formats for the user. Like mentioned before the project will not include any GUI development, therefore only two formats are provided: XML files and files using Gobo Eiffel test format [4].

Database query handler: The database query handler gives the user the ability to query the database. It is only partly implemented: it should be possible, at least, to retrieve the test results (more advanced functionalities are beyond the scope of the project).

Database storing: Storing into the database.

Demo application: The demo shows the functionality and scope of the *Test Wizard.*

Documentation:

Developer manual:	The developer manual documents the software architecture and its limitations, describes the difficulties encountered during the implementation and explains how to extend the current version.
User manual:	The user manual describes the usage of the *Test Wizard*.
Intermediary report:	The intermediary report consists of the intermediary developer manual.
Thesis report:	The thesis report consists of the final developer manual, the final user manual and a theoretical part discussing the profiling like the performance of the tool, comparing automatic and manual testing, etc.

2.1.3 BACKGROUND MATERIAL

READING LIST

- Chapters in OOSC2 [9] in particular:
  - Chapter 1: Software quality
  - Chapter 10: Genericity
  - Chapter 11: Design by Contract: building reliable software
  - Chapter 12: When the contract is broken: exception handling
  - Chapter 14: Introduction to inheritance
  - Chapter 15: Multiple inheritance
  - Chapter 26: A sense of style
  - Chapter 28: The software construction process
- Testing Object-Oriented Systems, Models, Patterns, and Tools [5]

2.1.4 PROJECT MANAGEMENT

OBJECTIVES AND PRIORITIES

Objective	Priority
Software architecture	1
Information handler	1
Test scenario handler (only implemented if time permits)	3
Code generator	1
Context handler	1
Context generator	1
Call simulator	1
Test result handler	2
Database query handler (only partly implemented)	2
Database storing	1
Demo application	2
Developer manual	1
User manual	2
Intermediary report	3
Thesis report	1

CRITERIA FOR SUCCESS

The criteria for success is the quality of the software and the documentation. The result may be a partial implementation of the objectives without implying any penalty on the success of the project.

Quality of software:
- Use of Design by Contract
    - Routine pre- and postconditions
    - Class invariants
    - Loop variants and invariants
- Careful design
    - Design patterns
    - Extendibility
    - Reusability
    - Careful abstraction

- Core principles of OOSC2 [9]
  - Command/query separation
  - Simple interfaces
  - Uniform access
  - Information hiding
  - Etc.
- Style guidelines
- Correct and robust code
- Readability of the source code
- Ease of use

Quality of documentation:
- Completeness
- Understandable documentation
- Usefulness
- Structure

METHOD OF WORK

The technologies involved are:
- Gobo Eiffel Lint [3]
- Programming language: Eiffel [7] (EiffelStudio 5.4)

QUALITY MANAGEMENT

Quality was ensured by:
- Weekly progress reports to the supervisor
- Detailed progress reports for each milestone
- Review of each milestone by the supervisor concluded by a meeting (see validation steps below)
- An intermediary report
- Documentation (see documentation below)

DOCUMENTATION

- Progress reports: Short weekly reports and detailed reports for each milestone will describe the progress and encountered difficulties to the supervisor.
- Developer manual: This manual documents the software architecture and its limitations, describes the difficulties encountered during the implementation and explains how to extend the current version.
- User manual: The user manual describes the usage of the *Test Wizard*.

10

- Intermediary report: The intermediary report consists of the intermediary developer manual.
- Thesis report: The thesis report consists of the final developer manual, the final user manual and a theoretical part discussing the profiling.

VALIDATION STEPS

The validation of each milestone comprises:
- **Report:** Sending detailed report and the relevant parts of the work to the supervisor for review.
- **Meeting:** Organizing a meeting with the supervisor for presentation and discussion of the conducted work.
- **Revision:** Revision of parts or all of the work for this milestone, depending on the conclusion of the supervisor.

2.1.5 PLAN WITH MILESTONES

PROJECT STEPS

Milestones	Objectives
M1	Software architecture: Design of the entire software architecture.
M2	Eiffel analyzer: Implementation
M3	Information handler: Implementation
M4	Code Generator: Implementation
M5	Context handler and context generator: Implementation
M6	Call simulator: Implementation
M7	Test result handler: Implementation
M8	Demo application: Implementation
M9	Intermediary report
M10	Database storing: Implementation
M11	Database query handler: Implementation
M12	Test scenario handler: Implementation
M13	Developer manual
M14	User manual
M15	Thesis report

DEADLINE

Milestone	Deadline
M1	2003-08-15
M2	2003-09-05
M3	2003-09-05
M4	2003-09-19
M5	2003-10-10
M6	2003-10-24
M7	2003-11-07
M8	2003-11-14
M9	2003-11-21
M10	2003-11-28
M11	2003-12-05
M12	2003-12-19
M13	2004-01-12
M14	2004-01-12
M15	2004-01-12

TENTATIVE SCHEDULE

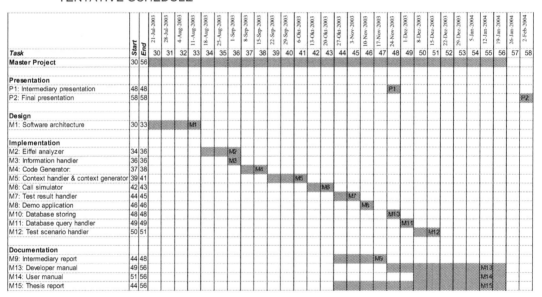

Task	Start	End
Master Project	30	56
Presentation		
P1: Intermediary presentation	48	48
P2: Final presentation	58	58
Design		
M1: Software architecture	30	33
Implementation		
M2: Eiffel analyzer	34	36
M3: Information handler	36	36
M4: Code Generator:	37	38
M5: Context handler & context generator	39	41
M6: Call simulator	42	43
M7: Test result handler	44	45
M8: Demo application	46	46
M10: Database storing	48	48
M11: Database query handler	49	49
M12: Test scenario handler	50	51
Documentation		
M9: Intermediary report	44	48
M13: Developer manual	49	56
M14: User manual	51	56
M15: Thesis report	44	56

12

3 DESIGN OF THE TEST WIZARD

The goal of this master thesis was to develop the tool *Test Wizard*, which generates test cases automatically from the assertions expressed in Eiffel libraries. As mentioned before the GUI development was not part of this project. Furthermore, all the database handling as well as the test scenario handler is not implemented yet. The project plan schedule and actual schedule are compared in the following table.

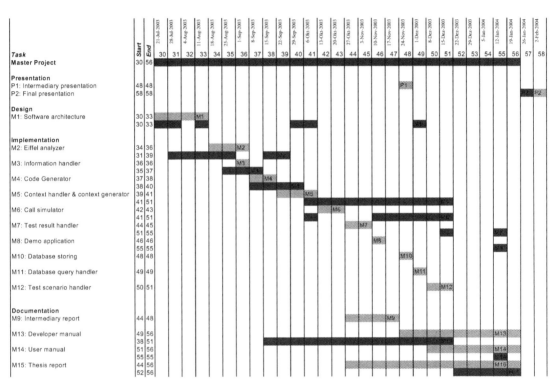

Task	Start	End
Master Project	30	56
Presentation		
P1: Intermediary presentation	48	48
P2: Final presentation	58	58
Design		
M1: Software architecture	30	33
	30	33
Implementation		
M2: Eiffel analyzer	34	36
	31	39
M3: Information handler	36	36
	35	37
M4: Code Generator	37	38
	38	40
M5: Context handler & context generator	39	41
	41	51
M6: Call simulator	42	43
	41	51
M7: Test result handler	44	45
	51	55
M8: Demo application	46	46
	55	55
M10: Database storing	48	48
M11: Database query handler	49	49
M12: Test scenario handler	50	51
Documentation		
M9: Intermediary report	44	48
M13: Developer manual	49	56
	38	51
M14: User manual	51	56
	55	55
M15: Thesis report	44	56
	52	56

Table 1 Planned schedule and actual schedule

Project plan schedule

Actual schedule

This chapter describes the actual design of the *Test Wizard* and explains the difference from the project description. Figure 2 shows the final architecture of the *Test Wizard*. The *Test Wizard* now follows a four-step process:

- Eiffel analyzer: Parsing the contract-equipped Eiffel library provided as input to get the system information.
- Information handler: Gathering user information to define the test scenario.
- Code generator: Generating and running the corresponding test executable.
- Displaying the results to the user.

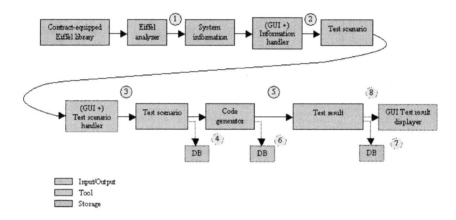

Figure 2 Actual architecture of the Test Wizard

(1)   Gather system information.
(2)   Display system information to the user and gather user information.
      Build the test scenario from the criteria selected by the user.
(3)   Adapt test scenario
(4)   Store the test scenario into a database (for regression testing).
(5)   Generate a test executable corresponding to the test scenario.
      Run the executable: it creates a pool of objects (the "Context") and performs feature calls on the pool of instantiated objects.
      Output the results to the users: generate XML files and Excel-compatible text files.
(6)   Probably store information about the test executable in the database.
(7)   Store the test results into a database.
(8)   Display the results graphically with diagrams.

3.1 EIFFEL ANALYZER

The Eiffel analyzer parses a contract-equipped library provided as input to retrieve the system information.

The Eiffel analyzer is implemented by the class *TW_ANALYZER*. It uses the parsing tool *Gobo Eiffel Lint* called *gelint* ([2][3]) to have access to the required system information. *Gelint* uses the tools *Gobo Eiffel Yacc* and *Gobo Eiffel Lex*. It is able to analyze Eiffel source code and report validity errors and warnings. The class *TW_ANALYZER* uses as input the universe (*ET_UNIVERSE*) generated by the tool. The generation of the universe takes place in the root class called *TW_TEST_WIZARD*.

The required system information is stored in an *ARRAYED_LIST* of *TW_CLUSTER*. Five classes are needed to store the system information, namely *TW_CLUSTER*, *TW_CLASS*, *TW_FEATURE*, *TW_TYPE* and *TW_OBJECT*. The Eiffel language [7] is taken as a model to store the system information:

- **Cluster**: a group of related classes.
- **Class**: the description of a type of run-time data structures, characterized by common features and attributes.
- **Feature**: an operation available on instances of a class. A feature can be either an attribute or a routine which is further classified into functions and procedures. Functions return a result and procedures do not.
- **Type**: Every type is based on a class, the type's base class.
- **Object**: Instance of a class created during execution.

The retrieved system information contains the list of clusters, deferred and effective classes, their generic parameters and descendants, deferred and effective features, their arguments and result types as well as modifiers and creation procedures.

3.2 INFORMATION HANDLER

The information handler receives the system information and enables the user to choose different test criteria.

The class *TW_INFORMATION_HANDLER* implements the information handler. The GUI development was not part of the project To highlight the changes between the project description and the actual development, I used the following marks:

- ✓ No changes
- Additional implementation
- o Not implemented

The user can set five test criteria:

- Scope of the test:
    - ✓ Clusters
    - ✓ Classes
    - • List of features
    - ✓ Features

- Exhaustiveness:
    - ✓ Number of calls performed on each feature:
        - ✓ Globally
        - ✓ Cluster
        - ✓ Class
        - ✓ Feature

    - ✓ Testing the same feature in descendants

- Context:
    - ✓ User-defined bounds:
      To define a bound, the user has to write a feature that returns the bound, a given type in a given state. Furthermore, he has to put the feature in a text file called 'bounds' placed in the directory also called 'bounds' of the *Test Wizard* delivery. Then, this file is put in the generated code and called during the initialization of the pool of objects.
    - ✓ Objects on which features are called
    - ✓ Creation procedure used for instantiation
    - ✓ Level of randomness of targets and parameters
      Fixes only the number of variants to be created, not the final number in the container (see Chapter 4.3.2).

- Tolerance:
    - o Allow rescued exceptions
      Can be set, but it is not handled.
    - ✓ Partial checking of assertions
        - ✓ Check instructions
        - ✓ Precondition
        - ✓ Postcondition
        - ✓ Loop invariants and variants (only both or none)
        - ✓ Class invariants

- Testing order:
  - ✓ Perform tests on one feature at a time
  - ✓ Perform tests on one class at a time
  - ✓ Test as many features as possible

3.3 CODE GENERATOR

The code generator of Figure 2 covers the code generator, the context handler, the context generator, the call simulator and the test result handler of Figure 1. Six classes implement the code generator: *TW_CODE_GENERATOR* *TW_CODE_GENERATOR_CONSTANTS,* *TW_CODE_GENERATOR_SUPPORT,* *TW_CONTEXT_GENERATOR_SUPPORT,* *TW_CONTEXT_GENERATOR* and *TW_TEST_GENERATOR*.

Figure 3 shows their dependencies. The first architecture proposed to generate the test executable at first and afterwards to establish the order and means to instantiate the needed classes. In my opinion it is easier to generate the code right from the start than to generate the code and change it afterwards. This is the reason why the architecture has changed.

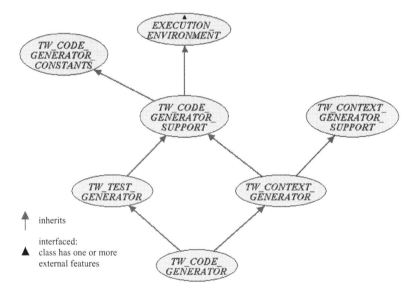

Figure 3 The class *TW_CODE_GENERATOR* and its ancestors

17

All classes used to implement the code generator are descendants of the classes *TW_CODE_GENERATOR_CONSTANTS* and *TW_CODE_GENERATOR_SUPPORT*. These classes offer constants and support features, for example features to generate common pieces of code like the **inherit** part.

The class *TW_CONTEXT_GENERATOR_SUPPORT* contains support features for the class *TW_CONTEXT_GENERATOR*. The class *TW_CONTEXT_GENERATOR* includes the code generator, the context handler and the context generator. I will call it *context generator* to simplify matters. It generates the file containing the class *TW_CONTEXT* that represents the pool of objects. Once the *context generator* has established the order and means to instantiate the needed classes, it actually generates the objects, and calls modifiers randomly on those objects to build the context.

The generated class *TW_CONTEXT* creates for each class a container holding objects of this class. The container is filled in three steps:

- Put one *Void* object in every container (respectively the initialization value for container of objects of expanded types).
- Iterate and create some objects of each type
- Call modifiers on the created objects

The duplicates in the container are deleted afterwards to avoid that a container holds the same object twice or even more.

The default creation procedure is chosen so that no current or pointer type is an argument. The object creation of base types and their associated reference type is treated differently. Predefined values are used to fill the containers. These predefined bounds are listed in Table 2. An exception is the class *INTEGER* which is filled with the values -1000, -100, -10, -5, -4, -3, -2, -1, 0, 1, 2, 3, 4, 5, 10, 100, 1000 and a few random generated numbers between -1000 and 1000. The reason why this class is treated specially is memory allocation. It prevents to allocate big chunks of memory (see Chapter 6.4).

Class	Predefined default bounds
INTEGER	-1, 0, 1, 2, min_value, max_value
REAL, DOUBLE	-1, 0, 1, 2, 3.14159265358979323846, -2.7182818284590452354
BOOLEAN	True, False
CHARACTER	'a', 'b', 'c', 'd', 'e', 'f'

Table 2 Predefined default bounds for base types

The class *TW_TEST_GENERATOR* includes the call simulator and the test result handler. I will call it *test generator*, because it generates the code for the test feature calls. A class inheriting from the deferred class *TW_TEST* is generated for every test feature. It

18

is also the *test generator* that generates this class. Exception handling is done by the class *TW_TEST*. All feature calls are wrapped into a rescue block to handle five possible cases: no exception, precondition violation, other assertion violation, other exception, possible catcall and void target object. Possible catcall is a new case that I will explain later. The case exception raised and caught internally described in the project plan is not handled.

The generation of the context and the test feature calls are independent. The class *TW_CONTEXT* offers access features *context_xxx* and *non_void_context_xxx* to the pool of objects. (xxx replaced by the class name including the parameters.) Therefore the test feature calls can already be generated, even if the context is not generated yet.

The ancestor of all these classes is the class *TW_CODE_GENERATOR*. It calls the Eiffel compiler, which builds the actual test executable. The test executable contains the necessary code to create the context, the pool of test objects, and the test calls.

3.4 TEST RESULT HANDLER

The test result is either passed, could not be tested, no call was valid or failed. The test result handler provides the result in two different formats for the user: Excel-compatible text files and XML files. The project did not include any GUI development, therefore a graphical representation displayed by the GUI Test result displayer is not provided. The files using the Gobo Eiffel Test format [4] are not provided either. The *test result handler* is included in the *code generator*, therefore no new class is implemented.

19

4 IMPLEMENTATION OF THE TEST WIZARD

This chapter describes the implementation of the classes described in chapter 3 and explains the implementation choices.

4.1 EIFFEL ANALYZER

The class *TW_ANALYZER* implements the Eiffel analyzer. The input is an *ET_UNIVERSE* created by *gelint*. The universe is created in the root class *TW_TEST_WIZARD*. The root procedure parses the .ace file. The needed scanner and parser to parse the .ace file is generated using *gelex* respectively *geyacc*. The parser generates an AST (abstract syntax tree) representing the constituants of an Eiffel class. The root procedure sets the error handler so that only errors and warnings are reported and it calls the feature *analyze_universe*. This feature sets the compiler to the ISE Eiffel compiler. Then the features *set_use_xxx_keyword* are called. They specify if xxx is considered as a keyword or just as an identifier. The tool sets **assign, attribute, convert** and **reference** as keywords. These four keywords are not part of the current version of Eiffel, but they will be included in the next revision of the language. The next commands (see Figure 4) called are equivalent to the different compilation degrees. The command *parse_all* corresponds to the compilation degrees 6 and 5.

```
a_universe.parse_all
a_universe.compile_degree_4
a_universe.compile_degree_3
```

Figure 4 Gelint: compilation degrees

The main class feature, *analyze_all*, puts the required system information in the structure *ARRAYED_LIST [TW_CLUSTER]*.

Let's have a closer look at the five classes that are implemented to store the system information and see how the required information is stored.

4.1.1 SYSTEM INFORMATION STORAGE

As the name suggests, an object of type *TW_CLUSTER* represents a cluster holding the required system information of a cluster and so on. I will call these objects in future *tw_cluster* not to cause a confusion between them and real clusters. This is also valid for the objects created from the other classes.

CLASS TW_CLUSTER

The cluster information is stored in the class *TW_CLUSTER*. It contains the cluster name and the parent cluster name stored in the attributes *name* and *parent* both of type *STRING* as well as all classes of the cluster stored in the attribute *classes* of type *ARRAYED_LIST* [*TW_CLASS*].

CLASS TW_CLASS

The class information consists of the class name and the name of the cluster it belongs to, the feature the class contains, the generic parameters if the class has any and all descendants of the class. It is also important to know if the class is deferred or expanded.

The class and the cluster name can be found in the attributes *name* and *cluster*, both of type *STRING*. All features of the class are stored in the attribute *features* of type *ARRAYED_LIST* [*TW_FEATURE*]. The modifiers are all features of the class without a return type (namely procedures). They are stored in the attribute *modifiers* of the same type. The default creation procedure is stored additionally in the attribute *default_creation_procedure* of type *TW_FEATURE*. The descendants of the class can be found under the attribute *descendants* of type *ARRAYED_LIST* [*TW_CLASS*]. The queries *is_deferred* and *is_expanded* give information about whether it is a deferred or an expanded class.

CLASS TW_FEATURE

The required feature information is the feature name, the class, the cluster name, the arguments and the result type of the feature. If the feature is a creation procedure or a modifier or if it is deferred, this is also part of the required feature information.

The queries *is_creation_procedure, is_modifier* and *is_deferred* are at disposal to check this information. The feature and the cluster name are stored in the attributes *name* and *cluster* both of type *STRING* whereas the class is stored in *associated_class* which is of type *TW_CLASS*. The arguments and the result type are stored, as the names suggest, in the attributes *arguments* and *result_type*. The type of the first attribute is *ARRAYED_LIST* [*TW_TYPE*] and the second is *TW_TYPE*.

CLASS TW_TYPE

The class *TW_TYPE* is used for the feature's arguments and result type. It contains the class name as well as the class and the actual generic parameters. Furthermore, the query *is_like_type* gives information if it is an anchored type. The class name and the class are stored in the attributes *name* and *associated_class* of type *STRING* respectively *TW_CLASS*. The actual generic parameter if it exists can be found in *actual_generic_parameters* that has the type *ARRAYED_LIST* [*TW_TYPE*].

CLASS TW_OBJECT

As the name suggests, this class represents objects, namely instances of classes. Every feature needs objects for its class and arguments. Initially instances of the class *TW_OBJECT* are not used, therefore the Eiffel analyzer does not deal with this class. Nevertheless, this class is used to store required information even if the information is just retrieved from the other classes described before. This is the reason why the class is already mentioned here. The object representing the class is stored in the attribute *class_object* of class *TW_FEATURE*. For the arguments the class *TW_TYPE* has an attribute *object* to store the object representing the arguments.

The class contains the following information: the associated class in the attribute *associated_class* of type *STRING*, the formal generic parameters as well as the actual generic parameters in *formal_generic_parameters* and *actual_generic_parameters* both of type *ARRAYED_LIST* [*TW_TYPE*], the creation procedure, the modifiers and the descendants. A special attribute of this class is *bounds*, which is of type *ARRAYED_LIST* [*ANY*]. It holds the user-defined bounds which will be explained later. Furthermore, the class contains the queries *is_deferred* and *is_expanded*.

4.1.2 CLASS TW_ANALYZER

The main feature of class *TW_ANALYZER* is *analyze_all*. First the feature creates an empty structure and then it calls the features *analyze_clusters*, *analyze_classes*, *analyze_features*, and *analyze_descendants* in order.

There are two access possibilities used by the Eiffel analyzer to access the structure *ET_UNIVERSE* that *gelint* produces. The first one is the attribute *classes* of type *DS_HASH_TABLE* [*ET_CLASS*, *ET_CLASS_NAME*] and the second is the attribute *clusters* of the type *ET_CLUSTERS*.

The feature *analyze_clusters* goes through all classes in the universe and gathers for each class the *tw_cluster*, namely the cluster's and the parent cluster's names. The *tw_cluster* is searched in the whole structure and created if it does not already exist. Afterwards the feature checks if the class is deferred or expanded, sets the *tw_class* appropriately and adds the *tw_class* to the *tw_cluster*. Finally, the *tw_cluster* is added to the structure, but only if it was newly created. Not every class is added to the structure, there are some exceptions. First of all, if an error occurred while parsing the class in *gelint*, secondly if the class is obsolete and thirdly if the class has only creation clauses that are not accessible from any class, except for expanded classes.

The next step is the feature *analyze_classes*. It just adds the generic parameters of the class using the feature *class_generic_parameter*.

The feature *analyze_features* goes through all features of the classes which are in the structure. It gathers each *tw_feature* that means the feature name, the associated class and the cluster name. The feature has to be exported to any class or has to be a creation procedure to be processed. In addition the feature should not contain any type of an obsolete class.

First of all the *tw_feature* is set to deferred if it represents a deferred feature. Then the result type of the feature is set using the feature *feature_result_type*. Afterwards the *tw_feature* is set as modifier, provided that it is not a feature of *ANY*, that the feature is exported to any class and of course that the feature does not have a result type. The next step consists in adding the arguments to the feature. To do that, the feature *feature_argument* is used. The feature *feature_result_type* as well as the feature *feature_argument* are using the feature *actual_parameters* to determine the actual generic parameters of the type. Finally, the *tw_feature* is added to the *tw_class*. If the feature is a creation procedure, it is treated in a special way (see Figure 5). In that case the feature can be exported in two different ways: first as creation procedure and second as feature of the class. The feature is added if it is exported to any class. The feature considered as creation procedure has another export status. If the creation procedure is also exported to any class, then a new *tw_feature* is created field-to-field identical to the old one, set as creation procedure and finally also added to the *tw_class*.

```
if is_creation_procedure (a_feature) then
        if temp_feature.clients.has_class (any_class) then
                a_class.add_feature (a_feature)
        end
        if is_creation_procedure_exported_to_any (a_feature) then
                a_creation_procedure := a_feature.standard_twin
                a_creation_procedure.set_creation_procedure
                a_class.add_feature (a_creation_procedure)
        end
else
        a_class.add_feature (a_feature)
end
```

Figure 5 Extract of feature *analyze_features* of class *TW_ANALYZER*

The last feature called is *analyze_descendants*. It adds the descendants to each *tw_class* using the feature *convert_descendants*. This feature is placed at the end, because it does not create new *tw_classes*, instead it looks for the *tw_classes* in the structure and just adds them as descendants, therefore there exists only one object for each class.

All required system information can be accessed by the structure *ARRAYED_LIST* [*TW_CLUSTER*].

4.2 INFORMATION HANDLER

The class *TW_INFORMATION_HANDLER* implements the information handler. The class takes as input the structure that contains the system information created by the Eiffel analyzer. The different test criteria are ordered by the feature clauses: Scope, Exhaustiveness, Context, Tolerance and Testing order.

4.2.1 SCOPE

The attribute *scope* contains all features that should be tested. There are four features at disposal to add features to the scope. The feature *add_cluster* adds all features of all classes of the cluster to the scope, *add_class* adds all features of the class, *add_features* adds all features in the list and *add_feature* adds just one feature to the scope.

These features do not only add features to the scope, they also set the query *is_in_test* of the features to **True**. This is later needed to create the context, the pool of objects to perform the test feature calls.

4.2.2 EXHAUSTIVENESS

The attribute *exhaustiveness* in the class *TW_FEATURE* determines the number of times the feature under test should be called. Class *TW_INFORMATION_HANDLER* contains four features to set the exhaustiveness: *set_globally*, *set_cluster*, *set_class* and *set_feature*. Using these features the setting can be done at several levels: for all features, for all features of a cluster, for all features of a class and per feature.

Furthermore, the class *TW_FEATURE* contains a query *is_descendants_set* which informs if the feature is tested in descendants. The Information handler provides the feature *set_descendants* to set this query to **True**.

4.2.3 CONTEXT

The attribute *context* of type *ARRAYED_LIST* [*TW_OBJECT*] contains the pool of objects. Four features are at disposal to fill this structure with the needed *tw_objects* to perform the selected test feature calls. Here the class *TW_OBJECT*, described before, is needed.

The explanation how the *tw_objects* are added to the context will start at the lowest level, the feature *add_to_context*. This feature simply adds the *tw_object*, but only if the object is not already included.

The feature *add_feature_to_context* (see Figure 6) adds to the context all *tw_objects* the feature needs. These *tw_objects* are the objects representing the class and the arguments. First the arguments that are of type *TW_TYPE* are represented by the class *TW_OBJECT*, i.e. the attribute *object* of class *TW_TYPE* is set. Then the attribute *class_object* of the class *TW_FEATURE* is set. This *tw_object* represents the class the feature belongs to. Now the class object is added to the context, of course only if it is not already included. Then the argument objects are added if the feature is in test. This query *is_in_test* was set when creating the scope. Furthermore, if a feature is under test and the feature has as argument a class with a formal generic parameter replaced by an actual generic parameter then this class is added with the actual generic parameter to the context as well. For example, the feature *fill* of the class *STRING* has the following signature: *fill* (other: *CONTAINER* [*CHARACTER*]). Therefore the *tw_object* representing the type *CONTAINER* [*CHARACTER*] is also added to the context. Finally, if a feature under test has as an argument a deferred class then the descendant classes are added to the context otherwise the base class of the argument is added. For example the feature *fill*: the class *CONTAINER* [*ANY*] is not added, but the descendant classes (like *ARRAY* [*ANY*]) are added. The argument objects are also added if the feature is a creation procedure or a modifier, but only if it is not a pointer, because the pointers are too difficult to create automatically. Therefore all creation procedures and modifiers needing a pointer are excluded from the context creation.

```
add_feature_to_context (a_feature: TW_FEATURE) is
            -- Add all objects that a_feature needs to context if not already included.
            -- add arguments only if a_feature.is_in_test, a_feature.is_creation_procedure or
            -- a_feature.is_modifier is true.
    require
            feature_not_void: a_feature /= void
    local
            arguments, actual_parameters: ARRAYED_LIST [TW_TYPE]
            a_class: TW_CLASS
    do
            a_feature.set_objects
            a_feature.add_class_object
            add_to_context (a_feature.class_object)
            arguments := a_feature.arguments
            if a_feature.is_in_test then
                    from
                            arguments.start
                    until
                            arguments.after
                    loop
                            actual_parameters := arguments.item.actual_generic_parameters
                            if not actual_parameters.is_empty then
                                    from
                                            actual_parameters.start
                                    until
                                            actual_parameters.after
                                    loop
                                            actual_parameters.item.set_object
                                            add_class_to_context (actual_parameters.item.associated_class)
```

```
                                    actual_parameters.forth
                        end
                end
                arguments.item.set_object
                add_to_context (arguments.item.object)
                if not arguments.item.associated_class.is_deferred then
                        add_class_to_context (arguments.item.associated_class)
                else
                        a_class := arguments.item.associated_class
                        from
                                a_class.descendants.start
                        until
                                a_class.descendants.after
                        loop
                                if a_class.formal_generic_parameters.count =
                                a_class.descendants.item.formal_generic_parameters.count then
                                        add_class_to_context (a_class.descendants.item)
                                        a_class.descendants.finish
                                end
                                a_class.descendants.forth
                        end
                end
                arguments.forth
        end
elseif a_feature.is_creation_procedure or a_feature.is_modifier then
        from
                arguments.start
        until
                arguments.after
        loop
                if not is_pointer (arguments.item.name) then
                        arguments.item.set_object
                        add_to_context (arguments.item.object)
                        add_class_to_context (arguments.item.associated_class)
                end
                arguments.forth
        end
    end
  end
end
```

Figure 6 Feature *add_feature_to_context* of class *TW_INFORMATION_HANDLER*

The next upper level is the feature *add_class_to_context*. It adds all *tw_objects* a class needs to the context. For efficiency the attribute *added_context_classes* of type *ARRAYED_LIST [TW_CLASS]* is introduced. This structure contains all *tw_classes* that are already added to the context, because it is senseless to check if every *tw_object* of a *tw_class* are already added to the context, given that the *tw_class* is already added. Therefore the feature first checks if the *tw_class* is already added, if this is the case the feature does nothing. If the *tw_class* is not already added, it goes through all features calling the feature *add_feature_to_context*. In addition, all descendants of the *tw_class* are added, if the query in Figure 7 returns **True**. This is the case either if a feature of the class is under test and the class is a deferred class or if a feature is set to be tested in descendant classes as well.

```
is_in_test (a_class: TW_CLASS): BOOLEAN is
        -- Is feature of a_class in test?
  do
        from a_class.features.start until Result or a_class.features.after loop
               Result := (a_class.features.item.is_in_test and a_class.is_deferred) or
               a_class.features.item.is_descendants_set
               a_class.features.forth
        end
  end
```

Figure 7 Feature *is_in_test* **of class** *TW_INFORMATION_HANDLER*

The highest level represents the feature *add_cluster_to_context*, it adds all *tw_objects* that a cluster needs to be tested. This is simply done by going through all the *tw_classes* and using the feature one level down.

It is possible for the user to define bounds. These user-defined bounds are directly added to the context by the feature *add_bound* (a_name: *STRING*; a_bound: *ANY*). To define a bound, the user has to write a feature that returns a bound. A bound is a given type in a given state. The feature written has to be put in a text file called "bounds" placed in the directory called "bounds" as well. Figure 8 shows an example how the file "bounds" could look like.

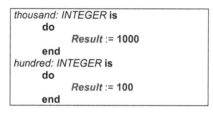

```
thousand: INTEGER is
      do
              Result := 1000
      end
hundred: INTEGER is
      do
              Result := 100
      end
```

Figure 8 An example file of user-defined bounds

The user only has to provide the name of the type, i.e. the class name, for the type he wants to define a bound and the name of the feature he has implemented.

It is also possible to replace the default creation procedure of an object in the context using the feature *set_creation_procedure*. The object class name and the new creation procedure have to be provided.

Furthermore, the level of randomness of targets and arguments can be set. It is defined in the attribute *randomness_level* and can be changed by the feature *set_randomness_level*. This feature sets the *randomness_level* to the new level wanted. At the beginning the *randomness_level* is set to the *Default_randomness_level* which is 1. (All constants used can be found in the feature clause Constants.)

4.2.4 TOLERANCE

For all different assertion checking levels, an attribute of type *BOOLEAN* is implemented. The attributes are found in the feature clause Status report and they are named as follows: *preconditions, postconditions, class_invariants, loop_invariants, loop_variants* and *check_instructions*. All of these attributes are associated with two features. If the feature names start with *set_...* then the feature sets the appropriate attribute to **True** meaning the checking of this assertion is turned on, otherwise the names start with *set_no_....* These features set the appropriate attribute to **False** meaning that the checking of this assertion is turned off.

The default tolerance is represented by a constant boolean that is **True**. All the assertions are set by default to the default tolerance, therefore full assertion checking is turned on at the beginning.

4.2.5 TESTING ORDER

The last test criteria is the testing order. There exist three testing orders that are represented by a constant integer:

- *All_testing_order* is 1:
  performing tests on as many features as possible
- *Feature_testing_order* is 2
  performing tests on one feature at a time
- *Class testing order* is 3
  performing tests on one class at a time

The default testing order, which is also represented by a constant, is set to *all_testing_order*. The attribute *testing_order*, which contains the actual testing order, is set at the beginning to this default value.

The feature *set_testing_order* allows to change the attribute *testing_order*. Only valid testing orders are allowed.

4.3 CODE GENERATOR

The *code generator* is implemented by six classes. The dependencies are shown in Figure 3.

4.3.1 SUPPORT CLASSES

The class *TW_CODE_GENERATOR_SUPPORT* inherits from the class *EXECUTION_ENVIRONMENT* to make it possible to change the actual working directory and to compile and run the generated code. All other classes implementing the *code generator* (except the support classes) are descendants of the class *TW_CODE_GENERATOR* and have access to all features offered by this class. The attribute *current_working_directory* and the feature *change_working_directory* are used to switch between working directories. For compiling and running, the feature *system* is used; it passes a request to the operating system to execute the argument of type *STRING*.

Two directories are created for the generated files: the test directory and the code directory. The feature *create_directory* either creates a directory or deletes the contents of the directory if it already exists. The directory as well as the directory name access can be found under the feature clause File access. The test directory contains all the generated files for the context and the feature tests; the code directory contains the .ace file and the root class.

The access to the test criteria fixed by the *information handler* is also stored in the class *TW_CODE_GENERATOR_SUPPORT*. The attribute *test_criteria* offers access to all attributes of the *information handler*, whereas the scope, the context and the system information are stored in the separate attributes *scope*, *context* and *structure*.

Furthermore, the class offers six features (see Figure 9) to generate Eiffel code used in every file like the indexing part. Each of these six features needs as argument the file that should be generated. The feature *generate_indexing* needs besides the description as a string. *generate_class* has as argument a boolean to know if a deferred class will be generated and of course the class name given as a string. *generate_inherit* has as second argument the class name of the inherited class. *generate_create* also has a string representing the creation procedure name. *generate_feature_clause* takes as argument a category, this string must start with '--'. Finally the feature *generate_end* simply creates the end with no further arguments. These features rely on the feature *put_string* of class *PLAIN_TEXT_FILE*.

```
generate_indexing (a_file: PLAIN_TEXT_FILE; a_description: STRING)
generate_class (a_file: PLAIN_TEXT_FILE; a_deferred: BOOLEAN; a_class_name: STRING)
generate_inherit (a_file: PLAIN_TEXT_FILE; a_class_name: STRING)
generate_create (a_file: PLAIN_TEXT_FILE; a_creation_procedure_name: STRING)
generate_feature_clause (a_file: PLAIN_TEXT_FILE; a_feature_clause: STRING)
generate_end (a_file: PLAIN_TEXT_FILE)
```

Figure 9 Features of class *TW_CODE_GENERATOR_SUPPORT* generating general parts of a class

The features of the parameter generation are also placed in this class, because both *TW_CONTEXT_GENERATOR* and *TW_TEST_GENERATOR* need these features. For the same reason, the features under the feature clauses Status report, Status setting and Search are placed in this class. These features will be explained later.

The class *TW_CODE_GENERATOR_CONSTANTS* contains the constants and keywords used in the generated code. Logically, they can be found under the feature clauses Constants and Keywords.

4.3.2 CLASS TW_CONTEXT_GENERATOR

The *context generator* builds the context, a pool of objects. The main features of this class are *generate_container_class* and *generate_context_class*.

GENERATION OF CLASS TW_CONTAINER

The first feature creates the file "tw_container.e" containing the class *TW_CONTAINER* (see Figure 10). It represents lists implemented by resizable arrays with the additional feature *purge_duplicates* that allows to purge duplicates in the list. The class *TW_CONTAINER* is used as a container holding the objects of the context. After the context initialization the feature *purge_duplicates* is called on every container to delete duplicates. The effect of this implementation choice is less control over the number of objects that the user has chosen by setting the randomness level. Therefore the randomness level just defines the number of creations, but not the final number of objects in the context. This implementation choice is justifiable, because after all, having an object twice or even more times in the context is useless. The feature *purge_duplicates* has a rescue clause. The reason of the rescue clause will be explained in Chapter 5.1.

```
indexing
        description: "Test_Wizard: Automatic generated file representing the container used by the context."
        date: "$Date: 2004/01/20 21:33:54$"

class TW_CONTAINER [G]

inherit
        ARRAYED_LIST [G]
                rename
                        copy as al_copy,
                        is_equal as al_is_equal
                select
                        al_copy,
                        al_is_equal
                end
        EXCEPTIONS

create
        make, make_filled, make_from_array

feature -- Purge
        purge_duplicates is
                        -- Delete duplicates in Current.
                local
                        failure: BOOLEAN
                        a_index: INTEGER
                do
                        compare_objects
                        from start until after loop
                                if failure then
                                        failure := False
                                        go_i_th (a_index)
                                        forth
                                else
                                        a_index := index
                                        if occurrences (item) > 1 then
                                                remove
                                        else
                                                forth
                                        end
                                end
                        end
                rescue
                        failure := True
                        print ("problems in purge_duplicates: %N")
                        print ("%Tclass ")
                        print (class_name)
                        print ("%N%Tfeature ")
                        print (recipient_name)
                        print ("%N%Ttag ")
                        print (tag_name)
                        print ("%N")
                        retry
                end
end
```

Figure 10 Class *TW_CONTAINER*

32

GENERATION OF CLASS TW_CONTEXT

The second feature, namely *generate_context_class*, creates the file "tw_context.e" containing the class *TW_CONTEXT*. This class creates the pool of objects needed to perform the test feature calls and looks therefore different depending on which features are tested. *TW_CONTEXT* is the most complex generated class and is divided in seven parts:

- Initialization

- Creation

- Modification

- Special bounds

- User defined code

- Container

- Access

All feature calls in the class *TW_CONTEXT* are wrapped in a rescue block, but the exceptions are not handled, so that the generated program does not fail generating the context. The creation and the modification are separated. Failing to create the object, simply because a precondition was violated in the modifier, is avoided by this separation. Furthermore, if one modifier fails to modify an object, another modifier is called. The selection of the modifiers as well as the arguments is random.

The feature *generate_context_class* (Figure 11) starts with assigning the files. These are the file containing the user-defined code for the bounds and of course the file "tw_context.e". All the attributes that handle the files can be found under the feature clause File access. The names of the files are also defined here as constants. The initialization of the structure *added_objects* takes place right after assigning the files. This structure is an *ARRAYED_LIST [TUPLE [STRING, ARRAYED_LIST [TW_TYPE]]*. The list is used to hold already added objects to the context to avoid adding an object twice. The objects are represented by their names and generic parameters. The generic parameters are available as an *ARRAYED_LIST [TW_TYPE]*. Two queries, *is_included* and *check_included*, and a command, *add_object*, handle this structure. The queries are to check if the object is already included, they just have a different signature. In fact, the feature *check_included* relies on the feature *is_included*. The command, as the name suggests, just adds objects to the structure.

```
generate_context_class is
          -- Generate context_file
    local
          a_directory: STRING
    do
          create bound_file.make (current_working_directory + slash + bound_directory_name
          + slash + bound_file_name)
          create context_file.make (context_file_name)
          create added_objects.make (0)
          a_directory := current_working_directory
          change_working_directory (test_directory_name)
          name_context
          sort
          fill_extra_scope_context
          generate_indexing (context_file,
          "%"Test_Wizard: Automatic generated file containing the context.%"")
          context_file.open_append
          generate_class (context_file, False, context_class_name)
          generate_create (context_file, "make")
          generate_feature_clause (context_file, "-- Initialization")
          generate_initialization
          generate_feature_clause (context_file, "-- Creation")
          generate_all_creation
          generate_feature_clause (context_file, "-- Modification")
          generate_all_modification
          generate_feature_clause (context_file, "-- Special Bounds")
          generate_all_bounds
          generate_feature_clause (context_file, "-- User defined code")
          bound_file.open_read
          from bound_file.start until bound_file.end_of_file loop
                bound_file.read_line
                context_file.put_string (bound_file.last_string)
                context_file.put_new_line
          end
          context_file.put_new_line
          bound_file.close
          generate_feature_clause (context_file, "-- Container")
          generate_all_container
          generate_feature_clause (context_file, "-- Access")
          generate_all_access
          generate_end (context_file)
          change_working_directory (a_directory)
    end
```

Figure 11 Feature *generate_context_class* of class *TW_CONTEXT_GENERATOR*

The next step establishes the order in which objects will be instantiated (see Figure 11). The commands *name_context* and *sort* put the objects in topological order. The first command assigns an integer code to every object that is later needed to sort the objects.

The class *TW_OBJECT* offers two attributes *name_code* and *argument_code* as well as two commands *set_name_code* and *add_argument_code* to assign a code to every object. The command goes first through all objects in the context and sets the name code for them using the feature *create_name_code*. Every time the feature is called it adds one to the integer stored in the attribute *actual_number* using the feature *counter* and sets the name code to the new integer stored in *actual_number*. Finally, every object is associated with another code. Then, all codes of the arguments of the creation procedure are put in the list *argument_code* provided that the object represents a class that has a creation procedure, respectively a creation procedure is needed to create an object of that type. This attribute is in the class *TW_OBJECT*. The sorting algorithm used is quite simple. It loops through the context and looks at the biggest argument code that is in the list *argument_code* using the feature *biggest_argument_code* of class *TW_OBJECT*. The creation procedure has an object as argument that is initialized later if this argument code is bigger than the name code. In this case the object is removed from the list and replaced in the list after the required object for the creation. Table 3 and Table 4 show a short example to demonstrate the sorting algorithm:

Class name	Creation procedure	Name code	Argument codes
ARRAY	make (min_index, max_index: INTEGER)	1	4,4
BOOLEAN		2	
STRING	make_filled (c: CHARACTER; n: INTEGER)	3	6,4
INTEGER		4	
DOUBLE		5	
CHARACTER		6	
REAL		7	

Table 3 Sorting

1. Create and set the name codes.

2. Set the argument codes.

3. Sort (see Table 4): At the first step the object of type *ARRAY* is put after *INTEGER*, because the creation procedure has objects of type *INTEGER* as arguments. Nothing happens at the second step because the class *BOOLEAN* does not have a creation procedure. At the third step the object of type *STRING* is placed after *CHARACTER*. The creation procedure of this class needs two objects, one of type *CHARACTER* and the other of type *INTEGER*. Since the object of type *CHARACTER* is created later than the *INTEGER*, this object is placed after that of type *CHARACTER* and so on.

35

ARRAY	BOOLEAN	BOOLEAN	BOOLEAN	BOOLEAN
BOOLEAN	STRING	STRING	INTEGER	INTEGER
STRING	INTEGER	INTEGER	ARRAY	ARRAY
INTEGER	ARRAY	ARRAY	DOUBLE	DOUBLE
DOUBLE	DOUBLE	DOUBLE	CHARACTER	CHARACTER
CHARACTER	CHARACTER	CHARACTER	STRING	STRING
REAL	REAL	REAL	REAL	REAL

Table 4 Sorting steps

The *information handler* already takes care during the creation of the context that all the objects that are needed for the test feature calls are in the context. Anyway, a few objects are needed and nevertheless not added yet. The next command *fill_extra_scope_context* calling the feature *fill_extra_context* repairs this. The simple reason that these objects are not added on the level of the *information handler* is that the *information handler* does not care about the generic parameters at least not in a strict way. This is only done in the *code generator*. The feature *fill_extra_scope_context* loops through the features in the scope and adds arguments of the feature to the extra context if the argument is a class with an actual generic parameter. Afterwards, the objects in the extra context are added to the context provided that the objects are not already in the context. Then the feature *fill_extra_context* is called. This feature relies on four features: *fill_extra_context*, *add_deferred_extra_context* and *add_extra_context* and *merge_parameters*. These features are not explained in detail because they are based on the features that handle the creation and modification of the objects. The pool of additional objects are stored in the attribute *extra_context* in each iteration of the feature *fill_extra_context* and afterwards added to the *context*. Before an object is added to the *context*, it is checked if the object is already included in the list *added_objects* to guarantee that no object is handled twice. The list *added_objects* contains all handled objects. If the object is already handled, then the object is removed from the *extra_context* and not added to the *context*. Then the feature *fill_extra_context* iterates again through the context as long as no more additional objects are found and put in the *extra_context*. The feature terminates if the *extra_context* is empty after looping over all objects in the *context*.

The first part of the class *TW_CONTEXT* is now generated calling the command *generate_initialization*. The command generates the creation procedure *make* of class *TW_CONTEXT*. The creation procedure consists of nine parts:

- Initialization of pseudo-number sequence using a default seed

- Container creation

- Creation of void objects (one void object for every container)

- Creation of an object of type *ANY*

- Creation of predefined default bounds for basic types

- Object initialization: creation and modification of the objects

- Creation of user-defined bounds

- Creation of objects of *ANY* using descendants

- Purge duplicates

The first part is simple. It just writes one line of code. It creates and initializes an object of type *RANDOM* and attaches it to the attribute *random*.

To generate the code for the following parts the schema in the Figure 12 is used: It loops through all the objects in the context and differentiates between objects of deferred and effective classes. Furthermore, it checks if the class is part of the scope if it is an object of a deferred class. A class is part of the scope if at least one feature of the class is going to be tested. The object is not handled if the class is not part of the scope. If the argument type of a test feature is deferred then it is replaced by an effective type in the call. But the feature *search_argument_object*, which is explained later, searches first the deferred object in the context and replaces it afterwards with an effective one. Therefore the object has to be in the context, but is not needed to generate the context.

```
from context.start until context.after loop
        if not context.item.is_deferred then
                ...
        else
                if is_in_test (context.item) then
                        ...
                end
        end
        context.forth
end
```

Figure 12 Context loop schema

The second part takes care of creating the containers. I will start with the implementation description of the container creation of objects of effective classes. The command *generate_container_creation* is called in this case. It allocates a container of type *TW_CONTAINER* with zero items for every object. The command relies on the feature *parameter_name*. This feature is used for the naming in the class *TW_CONTEXT*.

Three features, namely *deferred_parameter_name*, *parameter_name* and *type_list_name*, deal with naming. They can be found in the class *TW_CODE_GENERATOR_SUPPORT* under the feature clause Parameter generation. The name used in class *TW_CONTEXT* to represent the objects or the object containers includes apart from the class name also the generic parameters, so that the names are unambiguous. Table 5 contains a few examples of container and object names.

Type	Container name	Object name
INTEGER	integer_objects	context_integer or non_void_context_integer
ARRAY [CHARACTER]	array_character_objects	context_array_character or non_void_context_array_character
PROCEDURE [ANY, TUPLE [ANY]]	procedure_any_tuple_op_any_cp_objects	context_procedure_any_tuple_op_any_cp or non_void_context_...

Table 5 Container and objects names

The feature *type_list_name* has only one generic parameter list as input, therefore it can easily generate a string of this parameter list. The feature *parameter_name* has two arguments. The first argument is the actual generic parameter list and the second is the formal generic parameter list. If both the formal generic and the actual generic parameter lists are not empty then the feature calls *type_list_name* with the actual generic parameter list as argument. In the other case, if the actual generic parameter list is empty then the feature is called with the formal generic parameter list. Finally, the feature *deferred_parameter_name* has two arguments like the feature *parameter_name*. But instead of choosing one of the generic parameter lists, this feature merges the two generic parameter lists together. The feature checks for every formal generic parameter if an actual generic parameter exists replacing the formal generic parameter. In this case the formal generic parameter is replaced by the actual generic parameter. The three other features under the same feature clause do exactly the same except that they produce a string representing the Eiffel code for generic parameters. An example of the resulting string of these features are the generic parameters of the first column in Table 5. The following table shows two code extracts from the feature *type_list_string*. They show the handling of the formal generic parameters of the formal generic parameters. The class *TUPLE* is separately handled, because it is the only class that has a variable number of actual generic parameters.

```
a_parameter. ARRAYED_LIST [TW_TYPE])

if a_parameter.item.name.is_equal ("TUPLE") then
        if not a_parameter.item.actual_generic_parameters.is_empty then
                Result.append (type_list_string (a_parameter.item.actual_generic _parameters))
        end
end

if not a_parameter.item.associated_class.formal_generic_parameters.is_empty then
        if not a_parameter.item.actual_generic_parameters.is_empty then
                Result.append (type_list_string (a_parameter.item.actual_generic_parameters))
        else
                Result.append (type_list_string
                (a_parameter.item.associated_class.formal_generic_parameters))
        end
end
```

Figure 13 Code extract from *feature type_list_string* **of class** *TW_CODE_GENERATOR_SUPPORT*

The container creation of objects of deferred classes is different from the container creation of effective classes. The command *generate_deferred_container_creation* is called. The difference is that the container creation of objects of deferred classes creates containers for the descendants of the deferred class, but not for the class itself. An important query is *is_constraint_conform* to check if the actual generic parameters conforms under any constraint to the formal generic parameters of the descendant. This is the case if the class of the actual generic parameter is a descendant of the class of the formal generic parameter of the descendant class (see Chapter 6.3.3).

The next two parts, the creation of void objects and the creation of an object of type *ANY* are just done by writing one line of code for each. It just calls the features *create_void_object* and *create_any_object*. The generation of these features is explained later.

The following part, the creation of predefined default bounds also calls only the feature *create_xxx_object*. (xxx stands for the class name including the generic parameters.) Every object in the context is checked by the query *is_special_type* so that only the needed predefined default bounds are created. An object is a 'special' type if it is either a boolean, character or number type (see the first column of Table 2).

The object initialization includes the object creation and modification. The following code piece (see Figure 14) is generated for every object in the context, respectively for the descendants in the case of an object of a deferred class. The randomness level specifies how many objects of a certain type are created. Furthermore, the program does not modify any object in a container if the container does not have at least two objects. The containers are first filled with a *Void* object and therefore if the container contains only one object, it is for sure *Void*. These is the reason for the integer 2.

```
if xxx_objects.count <= randomness_level then
          create_xxx_object
end
if xxx_objects.count >= 2 then
          modify_xxx_object
end
```

Figure 14 Object initialization

An exception are the objects of type *POINTER* as well as objects of a 'special' type. They are not initialized in this part. These generated code pieces are in a loop that loops randomness level * 5.

The next part is the user-defined bound creation. It checks for every object in the context if the attribute *bounds* is not empty. This attribute is set by *the information handler* in the case the user has added a bound. If this attribute is not empty, the code line *create_xxx_bounds* is generated. The next line of generated code contains the feature call *create_any_descendants*. These features are explained later.

The final part of the creation procedure are the feature calls *purge_duplicates* for every container. It deletes duplicates in the container. This is the end of the initialization part of the class *TW_CONTEXT* that consists of the creation procedure *make*.

The creation is the second part of the generated class *TW_CONTEXT*. The command *generate_all_creation* called by the feature *generate_context_class* (see Figure 11) generates this part of the class. This command relies on eight features.

The feature *generate_void_creation* generates the code of the feature *create_void_object* of the class *TW_CONTEXT*. The correct name of this feature should be *create_default_initialization_value_object*, because expanded types cannot be *Void*. The following table shows the default initialization values of the different types:

Type	Default value
INTEGER, REAL, DOUBLE	0
BOOLEAN	False
CHARACTER	Null
Reference types	Void

Table 6 Default initialization values

Local entities are initialized with these values, therefore local entities are declared for expanded types. The query *is_expanded_type* is used to differentiate between expanded and reference types. All the containers are filled with an appropriate object initialized with the default value using *Void* for reference types.

The command *generate_all_creation* differentiates after the generation of the *Void* objects between effective and deferred types, type *ANY* and, on top of that, it distinguishes effective types between number, *BOOLEAN*, *CHARACTER* or reference types. Number types include the type *INTEGER*, *INTEGER_8*, *INTEGER_16*, *INTEGER_64*, *REAL* and *DOUBLE*.

The features *generate_number_creation*, *generate_boolean_creation* and *generate_character_creation* fill the container with predefined default bounds (see Table 2). The features *generate_creation* and *generate_deferred_creation* create the remaining features *create_xxx_object*. Furthermore, the feature *generate_any_creation* creates the feature *create_any_object* of the class *TW_CONTEXT*. Finally, the feature *generate_any* generates the code of feature *create_any_descendants*. It takes an object of every container and adds it to the container of *ANY* if the object is not **Void** or a default value.

The third part of the class *TW_CONTEXT* is the modification. The command *generate_all_modification* called by the feature *generate_context_class* generates this part. All the generated features are named *modify_xxx_object*. The command relies on only two features: *generate_modification* and *generate_deferred_modification*. The first feature creates the code for effective classes and the second for deferred classes.

The modifiers extracted with the help of the Eiffel analyzer are needed. They can be accessed by the attribute *modifiers* of class *TW_OBJECT*. Both features loop through the modifiers and handle them provided that the modifier is not a feature of class *ANY* and is not using a pointer. To check these properties the queries *is_any_feature* and *is_using_pointer* are at disposal. The features *generate_prefix_feature*, *generate_infix_feature* and *generate_feature* respectively *generate_deferred_prefix_feature*, *generate_deferred_infix_feature* and *generate_deferred_feature* are called to generate the code for the feature call These features can be found under the feature clause Feature generation. The feature names of prefix features contain the word 'prefix' and the feature names of infix features contain the word 'infix', therefore it is not a problem to differentiate the different kinds of features. The feature *generate_feature* is the most complex one, because it can have the highest number of arguments. The features to generate infix or prefix features have to handle only one, respectively no argument at all.

The feature *generate_feature* relies on the feature *search_argument_object* that looks for the right argument object and places it in the attribute *last_object_found_item*, furthermore it also sets the attribute *actual_parameters*. The feature as well as the attributes are in the class *TW_CODE_GENERATOR_SUPPORT*, because they are also needed to generate the test feature calls. The feature has three arguments. The first is the argument for which the object is searched, the second is the object on which the feature is called and the third argument is the descendant in the case that the object is of a deferred class otherwise it is just again the object itself. Therefore the feature can be used for both, to find argument objects of deferred and effective classes. A deferred type as argument is always replaced by an effective type. The object declared of the deferred type is needed, because of its actual generic parameters. To differentiate the objects, the object declared of the deferred type is called from now on *deferred_object* and the object declared of the descendant type is called *effective_object*. First of all, the actual generic parameters of the

41

deferred_object are stored in the attribute *actual_parameters*. The next step (see Figure 15) is to replace a formal generic parameter as argument by either an actual generic parameter of the *deferred_object* or a formal generic parameter of the *effective_object*. The command *search_tag_object* that relies on the command *search_parameter_tag* is called. It sets the attribute *last_class_found_item*. It compares first the attribute *parameter_tag* of the argument and the actual generic parameters of the *deferred_object*, afterwards it compares it with the generic parameter of the *effective_object*. If there is a match the replacing argument is found. In the case that the argument is not a generic parameter, i.e. no replacing argument is found, then the local entity *temp_object* is just set to the object of the argument.

```
if a_argument.parameter_tag /= void then
        search_tag_object (a_argument.parameter_tag, a_object.actual_generic_parameters,
        a_actual.formal_generic_parameters)
        temp_object := last_class_found_item.object_from_class
else
        a_argument.set_object
        temp_object := a_argument.object
end
```

Figure 15 First code piece of feature *search_argument_object*

If the object found is of type *ANY* and the actual generic parameters of the *deferred_object* are not empty then the object is replaced by the actual generic parameter (see Figure 16).

```
if temp_object.associated_class.is_equal ("ANY") and not
a_object.actual_generic_parameters.is_empty then
        a_object.actual_generic_parameters.first.set_object
        search_object (a_object.actual_generic_parameters.first.object)
        temp_object := last_object_found_item
end
```

Figure 16 Second code piece of feature *search_argument_object*

The next step is to replace objects declared of deferred types by an object declared of an effective type. The feature *search_effective_class* sets the attribute *effective_class_found_item*. This feature is implemented in the class *TW_CODE_GENERATOR_SUPPORT*. In the case that the object of the deferred type has actual generic parameters, they are kept in the attribute *actual_parameters*. The feature *search_effective_class* handles a special case. The deferred class *ROUTINE* should not be replaced by the class *FUNCTION*, because this class has one formal generic parameter more, the result type. That is why the class *ROUTINE* is always replaced by the class *PROCEDURE*. In addition, the feature takes care that the formal generic parameters of the effective class found conform to the constraint.

Finally, the attribute *last_object_found_item* is set when calling the feature *search_object*. Both, the feature and the attribute are implemented in class *TW_CODE_GENERATOR_SUPPORT*. The feature searches the object in the context and sets *last_object_found_item* to this object. In case the found object is of type *TUPLE* the feature is not finished yet. The class *TUPLE* is the only class which has a variable number of generic parameters. Therefore if the *actual_parameters* include the type *TUPLE* a new object is generated with the formal and actual generic parameters set to the actual generic parameters of the parameter *TUPLE* hold in the attribute *actual_parameters*.

The part containing the creation of the user-defined bounds is generated by the command *generate_all_bounds* that relies on *generate_bound*. In the class *TW_OBJECT*, there is an attribute *bounds*, the list of user-defined bounds. This attribute contains all feature names that the user has implemented. The code generated by this feature just assigns a variable to the feature and adds this variable to the appropriate container (see Figure 17).

```
create_integer_bounds is
                -- Create user-defined bounds.
        local
                integer_variable1: INTEGER
                failure: INTEGER
        do
                if (failure < 10) then
                        integer_variable1: := thousand
                        integer_objects.force (integer_variable1)
                else
                        print ("Couldn't create object of class INTEGER%N")
                end
        rescue
                failure := failure + 1
                retry
        end
```

Figure 17 Generated feature *create_integer_bounds*

The next part, the user-defined bounds, is generated by copying the file "bounds" that is placed in the directory "bounds", reading and writing one line after the other.

The remaining parts of the class *TW_CONTEXT* are the container and the object access. The code for the container access is generated by calling the feature *generate_all_container* that relies on the features *generate_container* and *generate_deferred_container*. The one for the object access is generated by calling the feature *generate_all_access* relying on four features, because there are two access possibilities. The first object access returns an object of the container whereas the second access only returns non void objects from the container. For every container both access possibilities are provided. For example, the modification of the created objects uses the

43

second access, so that the modifiers are not called on void objects. The non void access is generated by calling the features *generate_non_void_access* and *generate_non_void_deferred_access*, the other access is generated by calling the features *generate_access* and *generate_deferred_access*. The features that these features generates are used to access the pool of objects for the feature test calls. The features are called: *context_xxx* or *non_void_context_xxx* (see Table 5).

4.3.3 CLASS TW_TEST_GENERATOR

The main features of class *TW_TEST_GENERATOR* are *generate_test_class* and *generate_all_classes*, which relies on *generate_feature_class*. The first feature generates the file "tw_test.e" that contains the deferred class *TW_TEST* (see Figure 18), the others generate a file respectively a class for each feature under test. These classes are all descendants of class *TW_TEST*. All files are placed in the directory "tw_test". The place of the files is important to generate the .ace file.

```
indexing
    description:   "Test_Wizard: Automatic generated file containing the ancestor of all Test classes."
    date: "$Date: 2004/01/20 21:33:54$"

deferred class TW_TEST

inherit
    EXCEPTIONS
feature -- Run
    run (a_context: TW_CONTEXT; a_file: PLAIN_TEXT_FILE) is
            -- Call test feature call in a_file in context a_context.
            -- Set exceptions.
        local
            failure: INTEGER
        do
            if failure < 1 then
                    test_feature (a_context)
            end
        rescue
            a_file.put_string (associated_class_name)
            a_file.put_string ("%T")
            a_file.put_string (feature_name)
            a_file.put_string ("%T")
            if original_exception = precondition then
                    if tag_name /= void and tag_name.has_substring ("test_wizard") then
                            set_void_target
                            a_file.put_string ("void target object")
                    else
                            set_precondition_violation_exception
                            a_file.put_string ("precondition violation")
                    end
            elseif assertion_violation then
                    if tag_name /= void and tag_name.has_substring ("test_wizard") then
                            set_void_target;
                            a_file.put_string ("void target object")
                    else
                            set_assertion_violation_exception;
                            a_file.put_string ("assertion violation")
```

```
                    end
            else
                    set_other_exception
                    a_file.put_string ("other exception violation")
            end
            a_file.put_string ("%T")
            if tag_name /= void then
                    a_file.put_string (tag_name)
            end
            a_file.put_string ("%N")
            failure := failure + 1
            retry
        end
feature -- Test feature
    test_feature (a_context: TW_CONTEXT) is
        deferred
        end
feature -- Generate exceptions
generate_exceptions (a_file: PLAIN_TEXT_FILE) is
        -- Generate results in a_file
    require
        file_not_void: a_file /= void
    do
        a_file.put_string (associated_class_name + "%T")
        a_file.put_string (feature_name + "%T")
        if assertion_violation_exception > 0 or other_exception > 0 or possible_catcall > 0 then
            a_file.put_string ("failed")
        elseif no_exception > 0 then
            a_file.put_string ("passed")
        elseif precondition_violation_exception > 0 then
            a_file.put_string ("no call was valid")
        else
            a_file.put_string ("could not be tested")
        end
        a_file.put_string ("%T")
        a_file.put_integer (no_exception)
        a_file.put_string ("%T")
        a_file.put_integer (precondition_violation_exception)
        a_file.put_string ("%T")
        a_file.put_integer (assertion_violation_exception)
        a_file.put_string ("%T")
        a_file.put_integer (other_exception)
        a_file.put_string ("%T")
        a_file.put_integer (possible_catcall)
        a_file.put_string ("%T")
        a_file.put_integer (void_target)
        a_file.put_string ("%N")
    end
generate_exceptions_xml (a_file: PLAIN_TEXT_FILE) is
        -- Generate results in xml file a_file
    require
        file_not_void: a_file /= void
    do
        a_file.put_string ("%T<feature>%N")
        if feature_name.has ('<') or feature_name.has ('&') then
            a_file.put_string ("%T%T<name><![CDATA[" + feature_name + "]]></name>%N")
        else
            a_file.put_string ("%T%T<name>" + feature_name + "</name>%N")
```

```
                end
                a_file.put_string ("%T%T<class>" + associated_class_name + "</class>%N")
                if assertion_violation_exception > 0 or other_exception > 0 or possible_catcall > 0 then
                        a_file.put_string ("%T%T<result>failed</result>%N")
                elseif no_exception > 0 then
                        a_file.put_string ("%T%T<result>passed</result>%N")
                elseif precondition_violation_exception > 0 then
                        a_file.put_string ("%T%T<result>no call was valid</result>%N")
                else
                        a_file.put_string ("%T%T<result>could not be tested</result>%N")
                end
                a_file.put_string ("%T%T<no_exception>")
                a_file.put_integer (no_exception)
                a_file.put_string ("</no_exception>%N")
                a_file.put_string ("%T%T<precondition_violation>")
                a_file.put_integer (precondition_violation_exception)
                a_file.put_string ("</precondition_violation>%N")
                a_file.put_string ("%T%T<assertion_violation>")
                a_file.put_integer (assertion_violation_exception)
                a_file.put_string ("</assertion_violation>%N")
                a_file.put_string ("%T%T<other_exception>")
                a_file.put_integer (other_exception)
                a_file.put_string ("</other_exception>%N")
                a_file.put_string ("%T%T<possible_catcall>")
                a_file.put_integer (possible_catcall)
                a_file.put_string ("</possible_catcall>%N")
                a_file.put_string ("%T%T<void_target>")
                a_file.put_integer (void_target)
                a_file.put_string ("</void_target>%N")
                a_file.put_string ("%T</feature>%N")
        end
feature -- Name access
        associated_class_name: STRING
                        -- Class name
        feature_name: STRING
                        -- Feature name
        exhaustiveness: INTEGER
                        -- Number of calls
feature -- Name setting
        set_class_name (a_name: STRING) is
                        -- Set associated_class_name to a_name.
                require
                        name_not_void: a_name /= void
                        name_not_empty: not a_name.is_empty
                do
                        associated_class_name := a_name
                ensure
                        name_set: associated_class_name.is_equal (a_name)
                end
        set_feature_name (a_name: STRING) is
                        -- Set feature_name to a_name.
                require
                        name_not_void: a_name /= void
                        name_not_empty: not a_name.is_empty
                do
                        feature_name := a_name
                ensure
                        name_set: feature_name.is_equal (a_name)
```

46

```
                  end
        set_exhaustiveness (a_int: INTEGER) is
                        -- Set exhaustiveness to a_int.
              require
                        not_negative: a_int >= 0
              do
                        exhaustiveness := a_int
              ensure
                        exhaustiveness_set: exhaustiveness = a_int
              end
feature -- Exceptions access
        no_exception: INTEGER
                        -- Number of calls with no exceptions
        precondition_violation_exception: INTEGER
                        -- Number of calls with precondition violations
        assertion_violation_exception: INTEGER
                        -- Number of calls with assertion violations
        other_exception: INTEGER
                        -- Number of calls with other exceptions
        possible_catcall: INTEGER
                        -- Number of calls with possible catcalls
        void_target: INTEGER
                        -- Number of calls with void target object
feature -- Exceptions setting
        set_no_exception is
                        -- Increment no_exception.
              do
                        no_exception := no_exception + 1
              end
        set_precondition_violation_exception is
                        -- Increment precondition_violation_exception.
              do
                        precondition_violation_exception := precondition_violation_exception + 1
              end
        set_assertion_violation_exception is
                        -- Increment assertion_violation_exception.
              do
                        assertion_violation_exception := assertion_violation_exception + 1
              end
        set_other_exception is
                        -- Increment other_exception.
              do
                        other_exception := other_exception + 1
              end
        set_possible_catcall is
                        -- Increment possible_catcall.
              do
                        possible_catcall := possible_catcall + 1
              end
        set_void_target is
                        -- Increment void_target.
              do
                        void_target := void_target + 1
              end
end
```

Figure 18 Generated deferred class _TW_TEST_

The feature *generate_all_classes* loops through all features in the scope and calls *generate_feature_class* for each feature. The scope is a test criteria fixed by the information handler. It generates a class for every feature. The class consists only of two features: a creation procedure and a command. The generated creation procedure just sets the feature name and the class name calling the feature *set_feature_name* and *set_class_name* inherited from the deferred class *TW_TEST*. The generated command is the real feature test call. This feature is called *test_feature* and is already defined in the class *TW_TEST* as a deferred feature. Figure 19 shows the generated class for the call to feature *max* of class *CHARACTER_REF*.

```
indexing
        description: "Test Wizard: Automatic generated class"
        date: "$Date: 2004/01/20 21:33:56$"
class TW_TEST1_MAX
inherit
        TW_TEST

create
        make

feature -- Initialization

        make is
                        -- Set feature_name, associated_class_name and exhaustiveness.
                do
                        set_feature_name ("max")
                        set_class_name ("CHARACTER_REF")
                        set_exhaustiveness (10)
                end

feature -- Test feature

        test_feature (a_context: TW_CONTEXT) is
                        -- Call feature feature_name in context a_context.
                        -- Set exceptions.
                local
                        a_var: CHARACTER_REF
                        a_current_var: CHARACTER_REF
                        other: CHARACTER_REF
                do
                        a_current_var := a_context.non_void_context_character_ref
                        other := a_context.context_character_ref
                        if a_current_var = void or other = void or other.conforms_to (a_current_var) then
                                a_var := a_current_var.max (other)
                                set_no_exception
                        else
                                set_possible_catcall
                        end
                end

end
```

Figure 19 Generated class *TW_TEST1_MAX* for feature test calls

48

The feature *generate_feature_class* first checks if the associated class of the feature is deferred or if the feature is set to be tested in descendants. If one of these cases applies, then the same feature of the descendant classes is also added to the scope. The feature *search_feature* looks for a feature with the same name in the descendant class to be added to the scope. Therefore renaming is not considered.

In the case of an effective class, the feature *generate_feature_class* assigns the feature name to the local entity *a_string* to retrieve it later for the file and class name. The feature *class_name* replaces all tokens with a string, for example '|<<' is replaced by the string 'shift_left', so that the name only consists of characters. Furthermore, it appends at the beginning 'TW_TEST' and the *name_code* of the associated object. This guarantees that every file respectively class name is unique. Then the code for the creation procedure is generated. Finally, the code for the feature *test_feature* is generated. The code shown in Figure 20 differentiates between two cases: either the feature is catcall checked when calling it or not. It starts with assigning the attribute *arguments* to the feature arguments. The feature *set_arguments* and the attribute can be found in the class *TW_CODE_GENERATOR_SUPPORT*. A catcall is possible if the feature uses an anchored type as arguments. The anchor can be:

- an attribute or function of the enclosing class
- an argument of the enclosing feature
- ***Current*** (i.e. the current object)

To avoid catcalls the type information is checked during run time in the last two cases. First of all, it is checked if the feature has an anchored type as argument using the query *include_like_argument*, which relies on the attribute *is_like_type* defined in class *TW_TYPE*. If the feature has an anchored type as argument, it is checked with the query *is_real_catcall*, if it concerns one of the two cases that can be checked. Furthermore, features of expanded classes are excluded as well as features of classes that do not inherit the feature *conforms_to* of class *ANY*. This feature is used to check if the types are compatible. This feature is not exported to the classes *FILE_NAME*, *DIRECTORY_NAME* and *BOOL_STRING* of the EiffelBase library.

```
set_arguments (a_feature)
create temp_feature.make ("conforms_to", a_feature.associated_class, a_feature.cluster)
if include_like_argument and is_real_catcall
and not a_feature.associated_class.is_expanded
and a_feature.associated_class.has_feature (temp_feature) then
    ...
else
    ...
end
```

Figure 20 Generation of *test_feature*

The feature *generate_catcall* generates the code with catcall checking. This feature relies on *catcall_checking* that generates the code for every anchored type argument. The generated code checks the type compatibility for these types (see Figure 21).

Feature signature	Generated check code
deep_equal (*some: ANY; other.* **like** *some*)	**if** *some* = *void* **or** *other* = *void* **or** *other.conforms_to* (*some*) **then**

Figure 21 Catcall checking

To generate the code for the real test feature call, the features *generate_test*, *generate_infix_test* and *generate_prefix_test* respectively *generate_test_catcall*, *generate_infix_test_catcall* and *generate_prefix_test_catcall*. These features are written using the features from the feature clause Feature generation of class *TW_CONTEXT_CLASS* as a model, therefore they are not explained in detail.

4.3.4 CLASS TW_CODE_GENERATOR

The main features of class *TW_CODE_GENERATOR* are *generate_ace_file* and *generate_root_class*. As the name suggests the first feature generates the .ace file of the generated project. The tolerance that the user has chosen is put in action. It is a test criteria defined by the *information handler*. The .ace file has a default part containing the option section. The option *assertion* sets the assertion level of the Eiffel system. Table 7 shows the different assertion levels:

option	assertion level
check	check instructions
require	preconditions
ensure	postconditions
loop	loop invariants and variants
invariant	class invariants

Table 7 Assertion levels

The list of clusters in the .ace file contains of course the two directories "tw_code" and "tw_test". All the generated files are placed in these directories.

The feature *generate_root_class* relies on the feature *generate_processing*. It generates the file "tw_root.e" containing the root class *TW_ROOT*. The feature *generate_processing* generates the feature *execute*.

The feature *execute* first initializes the context calling the feature *make*. Then all the generated classes for the test feature calls are put in the container *test_container* of type *ARRAY [TW_TEST]*. The different testing orders are taken into account generating the feature *execute*. The feature are tested by calling the feature *run* on a class in the container *test_container*. The feature *execute* generates three different files: on "details.txt" file which is an Excel-compatible text file containing each error occurred during the test execution and the files "exceptions.txt" and "exceptions.xml". These files contain the same namely the summary of all errors and the test results. Whereas the first file is the same format as the "details.txt" file, the other is an XML file. This three files are generated using the feature *put_string* of class *PLAIN_TEXT_FILE*.

The different testing orders are taken into account with the features *generate_feature_testing*, *generate_class_testing* and *generate_all_testing*. The first feature generates the feature *execute* so that a feature is tested at a time. The second generates it in such a way that a class is tested at a time. The last feature which is the default testing order generates the tests in that way that as much features as possible are tested. This means that each feature is tested once before calling a feature a second time.

5 TEST OF EIFFELBASE

5.1 THE FEATURE *PURGE_DUPLICATES*

In chapter 4.3.2, it is mentioned that the feature *purge_duplicates* has a rescue clause. In fact this rescue clause has the same reason as all the other rescue clauses in the class *TW_CONTEXT*. They should prevent the program to fail during the context generation. It is more important to get a context at all than to get exactly the context we wanted. In fact the context is created randomly anyway. Therefore a container that contains an object twice is better than no container at all.

The feature *purge_duplicates* failed twice while testing the EiffelBase library. The problems were the containers of the *INTEGER_8_REF* and *INTEGER_16_REF* objects, both holding the object initialized with the *Min_value*. The minimal value is −128 respectively −32768. Calling the feature caused the invariant 'sign_times_abs' saying that an integer is equal to its sign multiplied by its absolute value to be violated. This invariant is wrong in the case of these minimal values, since the absolute value cannot be coded on this number of bits. For example the absolute value of −128 is −128 with these number of bits as well instead of 128. Multiplying −128 with −1 is 0 and not −128, therefore the invariant is violated.

5.2 BASE TYPES

The *Test Wizard* is not able to test base types respectively expanded types. Features that use an anchored type as argument can cause runtime panic if an expanded type is tested.

An example is the feature *copy* of class *ANY*. If the feature is called on an object of type *INTEGER*, it causes a segmentation violation. The Figure 22 shows the Eiffel code on the left side and the generated C code on the right side.

local
    int: INTEGER
do
    int := 30
    int.copy(int)
end
	loc1 = (EIF_INTEGER_32)((EIF_INTEGER_32) 30L);
	(tp1 = RTLN(RTUD(127)), *(EIF_INTEGER_32 *)tp1 = loc1, // int := 30
	(FUNCTION_CAST(void, (EIF_REFERENCE, EIF_INTEGER_32))
	RTVF(127, 14, "copy", tp1))(tp1, loc1)); // int.copy(int)

Figure 22 Feature *copy* of class *ANY* on expanded types

Xavier Rousselot commented on the generated code:

"As you can see, an INTEGER_REF is created on-the-fly to be able to call copy (which is normal). RTLN allocates the memory for the INTEGER_REF, it is assigned the value of 30, and then `copy' is called. Note that the second parameter of `copy' is an INTEGER, not an INTEGER_REF! This is completely wrong, because `copy' expects to be called with a real Eiffel object, not an integer. Therefore `loc1' is considered to be a pointer to an Eiffel object whereas it is an int!! And of course `same_type' fails (it cannot retrieve the type information on an object that does not exist). The funny consequence of this is that if you try to copy 0 into an INTEGER (int.copy(0)), you get a precondition violation on "other /= Void", which proves that the parameter value is completely misinterpreted! To sum up, this is a real bug, very well hidden, and I'm very glad the wizard found it!! :)"

To avoid this bug, expanded types have to be explicitly converted into the corresponding reference types before passing it to features with an anchored type as argument. The *Test Wizard* does not convert the expanded types, therefore base types cannot be tested.

Reference types can be tested. In the appendix you can find the results of the test of classes *BOOLEAN_REF*, *CHARACTER_REF*, *REAL_REF*, *DOUBLE_REF* and *INTEGER_REF* with the default testing order. The default testing order tests each feature once and starts then from the beginning continuing the testing.

The following two pop-up windows in Figure 23 can appear when testing the feature *infix* "^". These errors are not visible in the *Test Wizard* because calling this feature do not cause an exception in case of a domain or overflow error. Only these pop-up windows appear in this case.

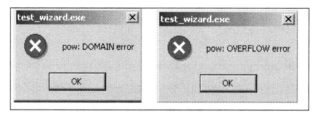

Figure 23 Power operation errors

5.3 NOT TESTABLE CLASSES

The *Test Wizard* cannot test the class *POINTER*. As a consequence, all classes depending on the class *POINTER* cannot be tested as well, unless the user provides some objects of type *POINTER*. It is not possible to generate objects of type *POINTER* automatically because the probability that the program crashes is too high. The context generation avoids as much as possible to use *POINTER* types. Creation features as well as modifiers that use a *POINTER* type as argument are excluded, if possible.

The deferred class *FILE* as well as the descendants of that class cannot be tested either. As a consequence, all the classes depending on that class cannot be tested either. The user has to provide objects of that type like for the class *POINTER*. Whereas the features of class *POINTER* are already excluded from the file generating the context, these classes, respectively their features, are still in the file. Therefore it is not possible to test classes concerned with the file handling at all with the current version of the *Test Wizard*.

Furthermore, the class *EXCEPTIONS* cannot be tested, because of the feature call *die*. The program terminates when calling this feature.

5.4 CLUSTER KERNEL_CLASSIC

This paragraph describes how to test the cluster "kernel_classic" of the EiffelBase library to give an impression how the tool works.

You can lookup in Table 10 that the cluster "kernel_classic" contains 43 classes. First of all, the base types cannot be tested. These include the classes *BOOLEAN*, *CHARACTER*, *INTEGER*, *REAL* and *DOUBLE*. Moreover the classes *EXCEPTIONS*, *FILE*, *PLAIN_TEXT_FILE* and *RAW_FILE* cannot be tested and the classes *POINTER*, *POINTER_REF* and *TYPED_POINTER* are not tested (see chapter 5.3).

Furthermore, two classes produces all the problems that the *Test Wizard* cannot handle. These problems are:

- Infinite loops
- Anchored types that refer to a feature and not to an argument or the current type
- Features calling C routines

For the class *STRING*, the *Test Wizard* encountered two difficulties. First of all, calling a feature that just calls a C routine and secondly an infinite loop in a feature. The first problem is caused by the feature *center_justify* and the second problem by the feature *character_justify*. This feature has an infinite loop, if the pivot used for justifying the string is not in the string itself. The feature *index_of* returns in this case 0 and remains 0. No matter how many empty character are prepended (see Figure 24).

```
character_justify (pivot: CHARACTER; position: INTEGER) is
            -- Justify a string based on a pivot
            -- and the position it needs to be in
            -- the final string.
            -- This will grow the string if necessary
            -- to get the pivot in the correct place.
    require
            valid_position: position <= capacity
            positive_position: position >= 1
            pivot_not_space: pivot /= ' '
            not_empty: not is_empty
    do
            if index_of (pivot, 1) < position then
                    from precede (' ') until index_of (pivot, 1) = position loop
                            precede (' ')
                    end
            elseif ...
            end
            ...
    end
```

Figure 24 Code extract of feature *character_justify* of class *STRING*

The class can be tested anyway, but the user must comment the features that cause problems out. In paragraph you can find the test results for class *STRING* without these two features. The problem that anchored types referring to another feature are not catcall checked appears in the class *ARRAY* [*G*]. The feature *is_inserted* causes runtime panic.

The appendix shows an extract of the test results. Most classes that should be excluded to test this cluster were mentioned before. Still, a few others needed to be excluded. (The generated project is adapted for the class *ARRAY* [*G*] and the class *STRING*.)

56

6 DISCUSSION

During my project I have gained a lot of experience in designing and implementing an Eiffel system and in using the tool *gelint*. To share my experience, I will discuss in this chapter the difficulties I have encountered during the design and implementation of the *Test Wizard*.

6.1 EIFFEL LANGUAGE AND EIFFELSTUDIO

I will start with the problems I had concerning the Eiffel language and EiffelStudio. The container classes only support internal cursors, but no external iterator. In case of several traversals of a list in the same time the consistency must be ensured. I used the class *ARRAYED_LIST* [G] for lists and noticed that an instance of an *ARRAYED_LIST* [G] had only an internal *cursor*. Therefore I had to adapt all my features that handle lists, so that they keep the *index*.

Furthermore, I have used the class *PLAIN_TEXT_FILE* to generate the code that offers all features needed. I only had to generate the code in order, because it is not possible to write in the middle of a file. At least, if you do not want to overwrite already written code. The advantage is that features generating the code can be read step-by-step to comprehend how the code is generated. The disadvantage is that I have to loop over the context for every part of the class *TW_CONTEXT* (see Figure 12).

Finally, I would have saved a lot of time, if it would be possible in EiffelStudio to run the program only without breaks caused by exceptions, above all if they are rescued.

6.2 THE SYSTEM INFORMATION

Classes for which *gelint* encountered a problem are not processed by the *Test Wizard*, because it is not possible to retrieve the system information correctly. For example if *gelint* found a syntax error in a class, the class should be reviewed first. The *Test Wizard* writes the class names to the standard output, so that the user has a list with all the excluded classes. Furthermore, the list contains additionally all the obsolete classes, because they are excluded as well. All the features that use an object of an obsolete type as an argument or result type are logically also excluded. The obsolete features are on the contrary tested.

6.3 CONTEXT

Which objects are needed to test a cluster, a class or only a feature? The first step is done in the *information handler* initializing the context. The algorithm used can be described as follows:

- Adding objects, instances of the classes that the user wants to test. They are either all the classes of a cluster, if the user wants to test a cluster, the class, if he wants to test a class, or the classes containing the features, if he wants to test only a few features.

- Adding objects, instances of the classes that depend on the objects added at the first step. They are all the classes used as arguments in the creation features, the modifiers and in the test features and the descendants classes of an argument or the enclosing class of a test feature, if the class is deferred.

To avoid an infinite loop the structure *added_context_classes* is introduced. It is checked if a class is already added to the context, before actually adding it into the context.

In the *code generator* the objects are sorted, so that an object that depends on another object, i.e. the creation procedure has the other object as argument, is created later. This is not really necessary, because the creation and modification of the objects is placed in a loop. If an object fails to be instantiated in the first loop iteration, it is probably instantiated in the following loop iteration, because the containers are holding more objects at every loop iteration.

The *information handler* does not care about the generic parameters in a strict way, therefore a few objects used as arguments are not in the context that is passed to the *code generator*. The *code generator* introduces an additional context. These additional objects are added to the context before generating the files. First, the feature *fill_extra_scope_context* loops through all the features in the scope. In the case that the argument object is a generic class with an actual generic parameter it is added to the extra context. Before the extra context is added to the context, it is checked again if they are not already included. Then it calls the feature *fill_extra_scope_context*. This feature loops through the context and looks at the arguments of all creation procedures and modifiers. Afterwards the extra context is also added to the context like in the feature *fill_extra_scope_context*. The feature loops again over the context until no more objects are added to the extra context. It is really important that the objects declared of deferred types are added to the context too, because the feature *search_argument_object* looks in the case of a deferred class for the object declared of the corresponding deferred type and replaces the class afterwards with an object of an effective class.

6.3.1 CREATION PROCEDURES

A creation procedure has two export statuses. The first one describes to which classes the creation feature is exported and the second one describes to which classes the feature is exported. It is not only a creation procedure, but also a feature. The export status of the features is not stored, because only features that are exported to *ANY* are further processed. Furthermore, the class *TW_FEATURE* has the attribute *is_creation_procedure* to know if the feature is a creation procedure. To differentiate the creation procedure from the feature, it is stored twice (of course only if the export status allows it). If not even one creation procedure of a class is exported to *ANY* then the class is excluded and not handled at all. The *Test Wizard* could not instantiate an object of that base class in this case. The *Test Wizard* chooses a default creation procedure that will be used to create objects of that type to generate the context. Naturally, only if the user did not change the creation procedure. The selection criterion of the *Test Wizard* is simple. It just takes the first creation procedure provided that the feature does not have the current or pointer type as an argument. A creation procedure with a pointer as argument is almost sure to fail. A feature with current type as argument would not produce anything interesting and it is even likely that it fails, too. For example the creation procedure *make_from_array* from the class *ARRAY* [*G*] has the argument *a* declared as *ARRAY* [*G*]. The only object that can be passed as an argument is **Void**, because that is the only object in the container before the creation part. The feature call would therefore fail, since the precondition array_exists*: a /=* **Void** of the feature would not be fulfilled.

6.3.2 MODIFIERS

Which features are suitable as modifiers? The features I used as modifiers changed during my project not only once. The first approach was to use all features that have the current type as return type as well as all features under the feature clause Element change. With the benefit of hindsight, this was not a good approach. To my defence, I had a look at the different classes and tried to find out which features are suitable as modifiers. The fact I used features with a current type as result type was because of the expanded classes. All the features doing an operation were included with this approach. For example all the operations, like *infix* "*+*" or *infix* "***", of the class *INTEGER* have as a result type an integer and modify the state of the object. But of course, considering the command/query separation principle only features with no return type should modify the state of the object. Therefore all features that have a return type cannot be a modifier. The second approach was to admit all features under the feature clauses Element change and Basic operations. The problem of this approach was that the *Test Wizard* should be language independent. Furthermore, there are no rules how the feature clauses have to be named. The final approach is that all commands are allowed as modifiers, i.e. all features without a return type, except the features of class *ANY*. The features of class *ANY* are excluded because features like for example *copy* and *print* are not really interesting. The disadvantage of this approach is that there are features used as modifiers that do not change the state of the object at all.

The next problem was how do I access the different modifiers. First, I thought about putting all the modifiers in a list using agents, so that I have the structure *ARRAYED_LIST* [*ROUTINE* [*ANY, TUPLE*]]. But it turned out to be not so easy, because of the infix features and arguments. Finally, I decided to use **inspect** instead. Figure 25 shows a model of the feature that modifies the state of an object of the class *XXX*. The modification features try ten times to modify an object. In the case that they do not succeed in modifying an object, a notice is written to the standard output, the console. The features choose the modifiers randomly using a random number and **inspect**. The modifiers are never called on void objects, therefore it uses only the *non_void_context_xxx* attribute.

```
modify_xxx_object is
        local
                failure: INTEGER
        do
                if (failure < 10) then
                        random.forth
                        inspect (1 + random.item \\ m)
                        when 1 then
                                non_void_context_xxx.feature_1
                        when n then
                                non_void_context_xxx.feature_n

                        ...

                        when m then
                                non_void_context_xxx.feature_m
                        end
                else
                        print ("Couldn't modify object of class XXX%N")
                end
        rescue
                failure := failure + 1
                retry
        end
```

Figure 25 Object modification

6.3.3 ARGUMENTS AND GENERIC PARAMETERS

I had the most difficulties with the arguments and the parameter handling of generic arguments. The majority of the compile errors were caused by wrong arguments and most of the time just wrong generic parameters of the argument.

60

A special case of the parameter handling is, if only one actual generic parameter replaces a formal generic parameter, but the class has more than one formal generic parameter. The parameters have to be merged together, i.e. only the formal generic parameter for which an actual generic parameter exists must be replaced.

First of all, the generic parameters of the generic parameters had to be handled as well. Secondly, the class *TUPLE* had to be treated in a special way, because it has a variable number of generic parameters. Another issue was the parameter handling, if an effective class replaces a deferred class. I also had to handle the fact that descendants of deferred classes can be deferred as well. Furthermore, classes can be inherited with an actual generic parameter.

For example the class *SEQ_STRING* inherits the class *SEQUENCE* [*CHARACTER*]. Therefore, an object of type *SEQ_STRING* can only be assigned to an object corresponding to the class *SEQUENCE* [*G*], if the generic parameter is *CHARACTER*.

Another problem was the class *FUNCTION*. The class inherits from the deferred class *ROUTINE*, but has one generic parameter more than this class. Generic classes with constraints were also an issue. A generic derivation is only valid if the chosen actual generic parameter conforms to the constraint. For example, if we want to replace an object corresponding to the deferred class *PRIORITY_QUEUE* [*G* -> *PART_COMPARABLE*] by the object corresponding to *LINKED_PRIORITY_QUEUE* [*G* -> *COMPARABLE*], it is not possible. The type *LINKED_PRIORITY_QUEUE* [*PART_COMPARABLE*] simply does not exist, because the actual generic parameter does not conform to the constraint (see Figure 26).

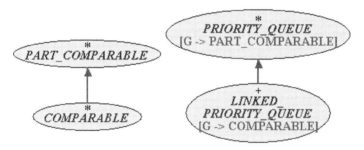

Figure 26 Constrained generic classes

6.4 TEST

Pointer handling was also a problem. Using a pointer that was generated respectively to generate a pointer is likely to fail. Therefore, no pointer type is used to generate the pool of objects. The user has to provide a pointer, if he wants to test a feature or to use a creation procedure with a pointer type as argument. This is done in the same way than creating a user-defined bound. Another problem is the file handling. The generation is also likely to fail, but this is not yet considered.

To avoid runtime panic caused by a catcall, the type information is checked at run time. A catcall is possible if the feature uses an anchored type as arguments. The anchor can be an attribute or function of the enclosing class, an argument of the enclosing feature or **Current**. To avoid catcalls the type information can be checked during runtime in the last two cases. Figure 27 shows two example feature calls. The first is a catcall and the second feature call works correctly. The feature *equal* of class *ANY* has the following signature *equal* (some: *ANY*; other: **like** some): *BOOLEAN*. The first call of *equal* fails, because the feature *is_equal* of class *INTEGER_16_REF* is used. The second call works fine, because this time the feature of class *ANY* is used.

```
any_1, any_2: ANY
int_16: INTEGER_16_REF
int: INTEGER_REF
bool: BOOLEAN
--------------------------

...
any_2 := int_16
bool := int.equal (any_2, any_1)
bool := int.equal (any_1, any_2)
...
```

Figure 27 Catcall

The catcall checking is done neither in features of expanded classes nor in features of classes that do not inherit the feature *conforms_to* of class *ANY*. This feature is used to check if the types are compatible. The feature is not exported to the classes *FILE_NAME*, *DIRECTORY_NAME* and *BOOL_STRING* of the EiffelBase library.

Another problem I have encountered are infinite loops and C routines. An example of infinite loops is given in Chapter 5.4. The problem of features that call a C routine is that they cause runtime panic if they fail, therefore it exists no possibility to rescue from the failure. The *Test Wizard* cannot deal with these two problems.

Features that allocates memory are also likely to cause runtime panic, if they are tested automatically. I have used two different strategies to prevent that features can allocate too big chunks of memory. The first strategy was to add preconditions to the features that allocate memory. I have done that with the features *make*, *resized_area* and *aliased_resized_area* of class *SPECIAL*. This new class *SPECIAL* can be found in the directory "extra_library". Naturally, the generated project is compiled again with this new class. The problem is that not only the class *SPECIAL* allocates memory. It is not only cumbersome to add the preconditions to all these classes, but it also impacts portability across compilers which do not have the same base classes. The second strategy was to allow only integer values between −1000 and 1000. The drawback is that the class *INTEGER* cannot be tested properly, probably also some other classes. Besides, a user can also allocate as much memory as he wants to.

7 OUTLOOK

I will discuss in this chapter the possible improvements of the *Test Wizard*.

A graphical user interface as well as a database should be added to the next version of the *Test Wizard*. The *Test Wizard* is not completely user-friendly at the moment. It would be nice to gather the user information through a graphical interface. A database would enable to store the test scenario for regression testing. Both the information about the test executable as well as the test results could also be stored.

Furthermore, the compiler path as well as the path to the "finish_freezing.exe" (executable used for freezing Eiffel code) are stored with the full path in the attributes *compiler_path* and *finish_freezing_path* in class *TW_CODE_GENERATOR*. These paths should be replaced by relative path names. Above all, the generated project is compiled by the *code generator*, but not automatically run yet.

7.1 CONTEXT

The exception handling in the context is not really advanced. In fact, the rescue clause is only to prevent the program to fail and the exceptions are not handled. A finer exception handling (already in the context file) would be nice.

The catcall checking is only done in the test feature calls, but not when generating the context. It could be added there as well. The catcall checking in the context would be part of an advanced exception handling mechanism. (I encountered difficulties with catcalls most of the time using features of class *ANY*. These features are anyway excluded from the context generation.)

7.1.1 CREATION PROCEDURES AND MODIFIERS

The *Test Wizard* could consider more than one creation procedure. The *Test Wizard* sets a default creation procedure in the current version. In fact, the user has the possibility to change the default creation procedure to another one, but the context uses only one creation procedure even if the creation procedure is changed. For example, the creation procedures could be called randomly like the modifiers. Another approach would be to replace a creation procedure only with another one in case the creation procedure fails a few times.

As mentioned before, there are still features used as modifiers that do not change the state at all. To avoid this, the code of the features could be analyzed to see which feature really alters the state of the objects. Furthermore, it would be nice to give to the user the possibility to exclude a feature as modifier. Even a list of features that are inconvenient modifiers could be stored in the database (naturally only when a database is added to the *Test Wizard*, but this is not the case at the moment).

7.2 TEST

The *Test Wizard* does not test features of obsolete classes, but it does test obsolete features. An improvement would be that the user can select if he wants to test obsolete classes and/or obsolete features.

The user cannot choose the actual generic parameters. Only the type *ANY* is used to instantiate generic classes. It would be nice if other types are used as actual generic parameters or even if the user can choose the actual generic parameters that he wants to use.

Catcall checking could be added for the case that the anchor is an attribute or function of the enclosing class. In the current version of the *Test Wizard*, the type information is only checked at run time if the anchor is an argument of the enclosing feature or **Current**.

Furthermore, expected output formats for future releases of the *Test Wizard* are a graphical representation as well as files using the Gobo Eiffel Test format [4].

8   USER MANUAL

8.1   INSTALLATION

To install the *Test Wizard*, please follow the instructions below:

- Download the package "test_wizard.zip". (The package is composed of the directories "librarybase" and "test_wizard". The first directory contains the file "librarybase.ace" which is the input of the tool. The second directory contains the directories "tw_analyzer", "tw_ast", "tw_code_generator", "tw_information_handler" and "tw_test_wizard". Moreover, it includes the .ace file of the *Test Wizard* called "test_wizard.ace".)

- Unzip the package in a directory of your choice on your disk and set the environment variable $TEST_WIZARD to that directory.

- Set *Compiler_path* and *Finish_freezing_path* in the class *TW_CODE_GENERATOR* appropriately. (These path names will be replaced by relative path names in the next version of the *Test Wizard*.)

- Download the package "gobo33.zip" and follow the installation instructions. Change the postcondition of feature *base_type_actual* of class *ET_TYPE* to

    base_type_actual_not_void: **Result** /= **Void**

    definition: **Result**.same_named_type (base_type (a_context, a_universe).actual_parameters.type (i), a_context.root_context, a_context.root_context, a_universe)

    named_type_named: **Result**.is_named_type

and   change   the   postcondition   of   feature   *base_type_actual*   of   class *ET_TYPE_CONTEXT* to

    base_type_actual_not_void: **Result** /= **Void**

    definition: **Result**.same_named_type (base_type (a_universe).actual_parameters.type (i), root_context, root_context, a_universe)

    named_type_named: **Result**.is_named_type

(This is already fixed in the CVS version of Gobo.)

The version 5.4 (or later) of EiffelStudio is required to use the *Test Wizard*. The assertion checking is otherwise not enabled and disabled correctly.

8.2 COMMANDS

The *Test Wizard* is delivered as a demo application. If you compile and run it with the file "librarybase.ace" as argument, the demo application tests the class *BOOLEAN_REF* of the EiffelBase library.

The *Test Wizard* is not completely user-friendly at the moment, because there is no graphical user interface yet. You have to set the test parameters in feature *analyze_universe* of the root class *TW_TEST_WIZARD* (see Figure 28).

```
analyze_universe (a_universe: ET_UNIVERSE) is
                -- Analyze 'a_universe'
        local
                analyzer: TW_ANALYZER
                info_handler: TW_INFORMATION_HANDLER
                code_generator: TW_CODE_GENERATOR
                a_cluster: TW_CLUSTER
                a_class: TW_CLASS
        do
                a_universe.error_handler.set_ise
                a_universe.set_use_attribute_keyword (True)
                a_universe.set_use_convert_keyword (True)
                a_universe.set_use_recast_keyword (False)
                a_universe.set_use_reference_keyword (True)
                a_universe.set_use_assign_keyword (True)
                a_universe.activate_processors
                a_universe.parse_all
                a_universe.compile_degree_4
                a_universe.compile_degree_3
                create analyzer.make (a_universe)
                analyzer.analyze_all
                create info_handler.make (analyzer.structure)
                a_cluster := info_handler.cluster_implementation (1)
                a_class := info_handler.class_implementation (26, a_cluster)
                info_handler.add_class (a_class)
                info_handler.add_class_to_context (a_class)
                info_handler.add_bound ("CHARACTER_REF", "character_m")
                info_handler.add_bound ("CHARACTER_REF", "character_n")
                info_handler.set_randomness_level (10)
                info_handler.set_testing_order (3)
                create code_generator.make (info_handler)
                code_generator.generate_container_class
                code_generator.generate_context_class
                code_generator.generate_test_class
                code_generator.generate_all_classes
                code_generator.generate_root_class
                code_generator.generate_ace_file
                code_generator.compile
        end
```

Figure 28 Feature *analyze_universe* of class *TW_TEST_WIZARD*

68

The commands available to set the test parameters are described in the following section.

You can set the scope of the test with the features listed in the following figure.

```
add_cluster (a_cluster: TW_CLUSTER)
add_class (a_class: TW_CLASS)
add_features (a_feature_list: ARRAYED_LIST [TW_FEATURE])
add_feature (a_feature: TW_FEATURE)
```

Figure 29 Features to set the scope of the test

These features need either an object of type *TW_CLUSTER*, *TW_CLASS* or *TW_FEATURE*. You can retrieve the clusters, classes and features using the queries shown in the Figure 30.

```
cluster_implementation (a_index: INTEGER): TW_CLUSTER
class_implementation (a_index: INTEGER; a_cluster: TW_CLUSTER): TW_CLASS
feature_implementation (a_index: INTEGER; a_class: TW_CLASS): TW_FEATURE
```

Figure 30 Features to retrieve clusters, classes and features of the library under test

The indexes needed by these features can be looked up in Table 10. This table shows the cluster and classes of the EiffelBase library. The classes *WIDE_CHARACTER*, *WIDE_CHARACTER_REF*, *CONSOLE, BIT_REF* and *RECURSIVE_CURSOR_TREE* cannot be tested by the *Test Wizard* because the wizard does not test:

- Obsolete classes

- Classes that only have creation procedures that are not exported to *ANY*

- Classes for which *gelint* encountered a parse error

The demo application uses the feature *add_class* to add the class *CHARACTER_REF* to the scope. The class is retrieved using the feature *cluster_implementation* with index 1. Then the feature *class_implementation* is called with the index 26 and the cluster just retrieved by the first feature (see Figure 30).

You can set the exhaustiveness with the features listed in Figure 31. Furthermore, you can specify whether a feature should be retested in descendant classes. The exhaustiveness is to retest no feature in descendants and 10 feature calls by default. The demo application does not set the exhaustiveness, therefore the default exhaustiveness is used.

69

```
set_globally (a_number: INTEGER)
set_cluster (a_number: INTEGER; a_cluster: TW_CLUSTER)
set_class (a_number: INTEGER; a_class: TW_CLASS)
set_feature (number: INTEGER; a_feature: TW_FEATURE)
set_descendants (a_feature: TW_FEATURE)
```

Figure 31 Features to set the exhaustiveness

You can set the context by calling the features in Figure 32. For the moment, it is required to have both the context and the scope set to the same clusters, classes or features. Setting a context that is different than the scope could be interesting when a database is added to the *Test Wizard*, but this is not the case at the moment.

```
add_cluster_to_context (a_cluster: TW_CLUSTER)
add_class_to_context (a_class: TW_CLASS)
add_feature_to_context (a_feature: TW_FEATURE)
set_creation_procedure (a_name: STRING; a_creation_procedure: TW_FEATURE)
set_randomness_level (a_level: INTEGER)
add_bound (a_name: STRING; a_bound: ANY)
```

Figure 32 Features to set the context

You can also change the creation procedure the *Test Wizard* chooses by default for a specific class. The feature *set_creation_procedure* sets the creation procedure using as arguments the class name and an object of type *TW_FEATURE*. Furthermore, you can set the randomness level which specifies how many times a feature under test is called. Finally, you can add self-defined bounds. You have to provide a feature for each bound written in the text file "bounds" which has to be situated in the directory also called "bounds". The demo application adds two user-defined bounds, namely the character 'm' and 'n'. The file "bounds" contains therefore two features, one returning the character 'm' and the other the character 'n' (see Figure 33). In the Figure 28, you see how these bounds are added using the feature *add_bound*. The demo application sets further the randomness level to 10 using the feature *set_randomness_level* and the context to the class *CHARACTER_REF*.

```
character_m: CHARACTER_REF is
                -- Create character 'm'
        do
                create Result
                Result.set_item ('m')
        end

character_n: CHARACTER_REF is
                -- Create character 'n'
        do
                create Result
                Result.set_item ('n')
        end
```

Figure 33 The file "bounds" of the demo application

The Figure 34 shows the features to enable or disable a certain level of assertion checking. By default, full assertion checking is enabled. The demo application does not disable assertion checking, therefore all assertions are checked at run time in the demo application. As mentioned before, to enable respectively disable the assertion checking correctly the version of EiffelStudio must be 5.4. (The assertion checking is defined in the .ace file of the generated project.) Loop invariants and loop variants are either both checked or both not checked. Finally, it is possible to allow or forbid rescue clauses in the test features. You can define if the feature call is considered as passed or not passed in the case that an exception occurred during the test execution and was rescued. However, this is not handled in the current version of the *Test Wizard*.

set_check_instructions	set_no_check_instructions
set_preconditions	set_no_preconditions
set_postconditions	set_no_postconditions
set_loop_invariants	set_no_loop_invariants
set_loop_variants	set_no_loop_variants
set_class_invariants	set_no_class_invariants
set_rescue_allowed	set_no_rescue_allowed

Figure 34 Features to enable and disable assertion checking

The tool offers three different testing orders. You can set the testing order using the feature *set_testing_order* (*a_order: INTEGER*). The different testing orders have the following meaning:

- Testing order 1: Performing tests on as many features as possible

- Testing order 2: Performing tests on one feature at a time

- Testing order 3: Performing tests on one class at a time

The demo application sets the testing order to the second testing order (see Figure 28), therefore the features are tested one after the other.

8.3 LAUNCH THE GENERATED PROJECT

Once you have set all parameters, you can launch the tool. The *Test Wizard* generates another project and compiles it. Unfortunately it is not possible to run the generated project within the *Test Wizard* yet. Therefore you have to run the generated program which is generated in the directory "tw_code". This directory contains the root class and the .ace file besides the compiled program. All the other files of the program are generated in the directory "tw_test". This directory contains a class for each feature under test as well as the class *TW_CONTEXT* and the deferred class *TW_TEST*.

The generated program generates three different files: Two Excel-compatible text files called "details.txt" (see Table 8) and "exceptions.txt" (see Table 9) and an XML file called "exceptions.xml" (see Figure 35). The generated program writes a line into the file "details.txt" each time a test feature call did not work. The written line contains the class and the feature name, the kind of exception and the associated tag for assertion violations. The file "exceptions" is provided in two different formats. They are generated after the test feature calls. They contain the summary of all the exceptions as well as the result. The possible results are:

- passed

- could not be tested

- no call was valid

- failed

class	feature	kind	tag
CHARACTER_REF	is_equal	precondition violation	other_not_void
CHARACTER_REF	is_equal	precondition violation	other_not_void
CHARACTER_REF	three_way_comparison	precondition violation	other_exists
CHARACTER_REF	infix "+"	precondition violation	valid_increment
CHARACTER_REF	infix "+"	precondition violation	valid_increment
CHARACTER_REF	infix "+"	precondition violation	valid_increment
CHARACTER_REF	infix "+"	precondition violation	valid_increment
CHARACTER_REF	infix "+"	precondition violation	valid_increment
CHARACTER_REF	infix "-"	precondition violation	valid_decrement
CHARACTER_REF	infix "-"	precondition violation	valid_decrement
CHARACTER_REF	infix "-"	precondition violation	valid_decrement
CHARACTER_REF	infix "-"	precondition violation	valid_decrement
CHARACTER_REF	infix ">"	precondition violation	other_exists
CHARACTER_REF	infix ">"	precondition violation	other_exists
CHARACTER_REF	max	precondition violation	other_exists
CHARACTER_REF	min	precondition violation	other_exists
CHARACTER_REF	min	precondition violation	other_exists
CHARACTER_REF	min	precondition violation	other_exists
CHARACTER_REF	conforms_to	precondition violation	other_not_void
CHARACTER_REF	same_type	precondition violation	other_not_void
CHARACTER_REF	copy	precondition violation	other_not_void

Table 8 The file „details" generated testing the class *CHARACTER_REF*

class	feature	result	no exception	precondition violation	assertion violation	other exception	possible catcall	void target object
CHARACTER_REF	item	passed	10	0	0	0	0	0
CHARACTER_REF	code	passed	10	0	0	0	0	0
CHARACTER_REF	hash_code	passed	10	0	0	0	0	0
CHARACTER_REF	Min_value	passed	10	0	0	0	0	0
CHARACTER_REF	Max_value	passed	10	0	0	0	0	0
CHARACTER_REF	is_hashable	passed	10	0	0	0	0	0
CHARACTER_REF	infix "<"	passed	10	0	0	0	0	0
CHARACTER_REF	is_equal	passed	8	2	0	0	0	0
CHARACTER_REF	three_way_comparison	passed	9	1	0	0	0	0
CHARACTER_REF	infix "+"	passed	5	5	0	0	0	0
CHARACTER_REF	infix "-"	passed	6	4	0	0	0	0
CHARACTER_REF	infix "|-|"	passed	10	0	0	0	0	0
CHARACTER_REF	next	passed	10	0	0	0	0	0
CHARACTER_REF	previous	passed	10	0	0	0	0	0
CHARACTER_REF	set_item	passed	10	0	0	0	0	0
CHARACTER_REF	out	passed	10	0	0	0	0	0
CHARACTER_REF	as_upper	passed	10	0	0	0	0	0
CHARACTER_REF	upper	passed	10	0	0	0	0	0
CHARACTER_REF	as_lower	passed	10	0	0	0	0	0
CHARACTER_REF	lower	passed	10	0	0	0	0	0
CHARACTER_REF	is_lower	passed	10	0	0	0	0	0
CHARACTER_REF	is_upper	passed	10	0	0	0	0	0
CHARACTER_REF	is_digit	passed	10	0	0	0	0	0
CHARACTER_REF	is_alpha	passed	10	0	0	0	0	0
CHARACTER_REF	infix "<="	passed	10	0	0	0	0	0
CHARACTER_REF	infix ">"	passed	8	2	0	0	0	0
CHARACTER_REF	infix ">="	passed	10	0	0	0	0	0
CHARACTER_REF	max	passed	9	1	0	0	0	0
CHARACTER_REF	min	passed	7	3	0	0	0	0
CHARACTER_REF	generator	passed	10	0	0	0	0	0
CHARACTER_REF	generating_type	passed	10	0	0	0	0	0
CHARACTER_REF	conforms_to	passed	9	1	0	0	0	0
CHARACTER_REF	same_type	passed	9	1	0	0	0	0
CHARACTER_REF	consistent	passed	10	0	0	0	0	0
CHARACTER_REF	standard_is_equal	passed	10	0	0	0	0	0
CHARACTER_REF	equal	failed	4	0	0	0	6	0
CHARACTER_REF	standard_equal	failed	7	0	0	0	3	0
CHARACTER_REF	deep_equal	failed	7	0	0	0	3	0
CHARACTER_REF	copy	passed	9	1	0	0	0	0
CHARACTER_REF	standard_copy	passed	10	0	0	0	0	0
CHARACTER_REF	clone	passed	10	0	0	0	0	0
CHARACTER_REF	standard_clone	passed	10	0	0	0	0	0
CHARACTER_REF	standard_twin	passed	10	0	0	0	0	0
CHARACTER_REF	deep_clone	passed	10	0	0	0	0	0
CHARACTER_REF	deep_copy	passed	10	0	0	0	0	0
CHARACTER_REF	setup	passed	10	0	0	0	0	0
CHARACTER_REF	io	passed	10	0	0	0	0	0
CHARACTER_REF	tagged_out	passed	10	0	0	0	0	0
CHARACTER_REF	print	passed	10	0	0	0	0	0
CHARACTER_REF	Operating_environment	passed	10	0	0	0	0	0
CHARACTER_REF	default_rescue	passed	10	0	0	0	0	0
CHARACTER_REF	default_create	passed	10	0	0	0	0	0
CHARACTER_REF	do_nothing	passed	10	0	0	0	0	0
CHARACTER_REF	default	passed	10	0	0	0	0	0
CHARACTER_REF	default_pointer	passed	10	0	0	0	0	0
CHARACTER_REF	Void	passed	10	0	0	0	0	0

Table 9 Test results of testing the class *CHARACTER_REF*

```xml
<?xml version="1.0" encoding="ISO8859-1" ?>
<test_results>
  <feature>
      <name>item</name>
      <class>CHARACTER_REF</class>
      <result>passed</result>
      <no_exception>10</no_exception>
      <precondition_violation>0</precondition_violation>
      <assertion_violation>0</assertion_violation>
      <other_exception>0</other_exception>
      <possible_catcall>0</possible_catcall>
      <void_target>0</void_target>
  </feature>
  <feature>
      <name>code</name>
      <class>CHARACTER_REF</class>
      <result>passed</result>
      <no_exception>10</no_exception>
      <precondition_violation>0</precondition_violation>
      <assertion_violation>0</assertion_violation>
      <other_exception>0</other_exception>
      <possible_catcall>0</possible_catcall>
      <void_target>0</void_target>
  </feature>
...

  <feature>
      <name>default_pointer</name>
      <class>CHARACTER_REF</class>
      <result>passed</result>
      <no_exception>10</no_exception>
      <precondition_violation>0</precondition_violation>
      <assertion_violation>0</assertion_violation>
      <other_exception>0</other_exception>
      <possible_catcall>0</possible_catcall>
      <void_target>0</void_target>
  </feature>
  <feature>
      <name>Void</name>
      <class>CHARACTER_REF</class>
      <result>passed</result>
      <no_exception>10</no_exception>
      <precondition_violation>0</precondition_violation>
      <assertion_violation>0</assertion_violation>
      <other_exception>0</other_exception>
      <possible_catcall>0</possible_catcall>
      <void_target>0</void_target>
  </feature>
</test_results>
```

Figure 35 Extract of the test results of testing the class *CHARACTER_REF* in XML format

9 APPENDIX

9.1 CLUSTER AND CLASSES OF THE LIBRARY EIFFELBASE

1. kernel_classic					
1. ANY	2. TUPLE	3. STRING	4. ARRAY	5. BOOLEAN	6. CHARACTER
7. INTEGER	8. INTEGER_8	9. INTEGER_16	10. INTEGER_64	11. REAL	12.DOUBLE
13. POINTER	14. DOUBLE_REF	15. REAL_REF	16. PLATFORM	17. MEMORY	18.SPECIAL
19. FUNCTION	20. PLAIN_TEXT_FILE	21. UNIX_SIGNALS	22. GC_INFO	23. FILE	24.POINTER_REF
25. ROUTINE	26. CHARACTER_REF	27. BOOLEAN_REF	28. ARGUMENTS	29. ISE_RUNTIME	30.MEM_INFO
31. RAW_FILE	32. STREAM	33. DECLARATOR	34. DIRECTORY_NAME	35. PATH_NAME	36.STORABLE
37. EXCEPTIONS	38. UNIX_FILE_INFO	39. BASIC_ROUTINES	40. PROCEDURE	41. DIRECTORY	42.FILE_NAME
43. TYPED_POINTER					
2. no cluster					
1. GENERAL	2. NONE	3. BIT			
3. kernel					
1. INTEGER_REF	2. NUMERIC	3. COMPARABLE	4. HASHABLE	5. INTEGER_INTERVAL	6. PART_COMPARABLE
7. MEM_CONST	8. IO_MEDIUM	9. STRING_HANDLER	10. EXCEP_CONST	11. INTEGER_64_REF	12.TO_SPECIAL
13. SEQ_STRING	14. STD_FILES	15. INTEGER_16_REF	16. INTEGER_8_REF		
4. list					
1. SEQUENCE	2. ARRAYED_LIST	3. LIST	4. BI_LINKABLE	5. LINKABLE	6. LINKED_LIST
7. SORTED_TWO_WAY_LIST	8. CHAIN	9. DYNAMIC_LIST	10. TWO_WAY_LIST	11. TWO_WAY_CIRCULAR	12.LINKED_CIRCULAR
13. SORTED_LIST	14. FIXED_LIST	15. DYNAMIC_CIRCULAR	16. CIRCULAR	17. DYNAMIC_CHAIN	18.ARRAYED_CIRCULAR
19. PART_SORTED_LIST	20. CELL	21. MULTI_ARRAY_LIST	22. PART_SORTED_TWO_WAY_LIST		
5. cursors					
1. CURSOR	2. ARRAYED_LIST_CURSOR	3. COMPACT_TREE_CURSOR	4. LINKED_TREE_CURSOR	5. HASH_TABLE_CURSOR	6. CIRCULAR_CURSOR
7. TWO_WAY_TREE_CURSOR	8. MULTAR_LIST_CURSOR	9. LINKED_LIST_CURSOR			
6. storage					
1. RESIZABLE	2. UNBOUNDED	3. COUNTABLE	4. BOUNDED	5. FINITE	6. FIXED
7. INFINITE	8. BOX				
7. access					
1. INDEXABLE	2. ACTIVE	3. BAG	4. COLLECTION	5. CURSOR_STRUCTURE	6. CONTAINER
7. TABLE					
8. set					
1. SET	2. LINKED_SET	3. LINEAR_SUBSET	4. PART_SORTED_SET	5. TRAVERSABLE_SUBSET	6. BINARY_SEARCH_TREE_SET
7. COMPARABLE_SET	8. ARRAYED_SET	9. SUBSET	10. TWO_WAY_SORTED_SET		
9. traversing					
1. LINEAR	2. HIERARCHICAL	3. TRAVERSABLE	4. BILINEAR		
10. support					
1. DEBUG_OUTPUT	2. MEMORY_STRUCTURE	3. MISMATCH_CORRECTOR	4. PRIMES	5. RANDOM	6. COUNTABLE_SEQUENCE
7. FIBONACCI	8. FORMAT_INTEGER	9. MEMORY_STREAM	10. ASCII	11.MATH_CONST	12.FORMAT_DOUBLE
13. C_STRING					
11. support_classic					
1. INTERNAL	2. OPERATING_ENVIRONMENT	3. DOUBLE_MATH	4. MANAGED_POINTER	5. MISMATCH_INFORMATION	6. BOOL_STRING
7. IDENTIFIED	8. PROFILING_SETTING	9. EXECUTION_ENVIRONMENT	10. IDENTIFIED_CONTROLLER	11.SINGLE_MATH	12.CLASS_NAME_TRANSLATIONS

12. table					
1. HASH_TABLE	2. ARRAY2				

13. tree					
1. DYNAMIC_TREE	2. LINKED_TREE	3. TWO_WAY_TREE	4. BINARY SEARCH_TREE	5. TREE	6. BINARY_TREE
7. FIXED_TREE	8. ARRAYED_TREE				

14. cursor_tree					
1. TWO_WAY_ CURSOR_TREE	2. RECURSIVE _CURSOR_TREE	3. CURSOR_TREE	4. LINKED _CURSOR_TREE	5. COMPACT _CURSOR_TREE	

15. dispenser					
1. LINKED_STACK	2. STACK	3. LINKED PRIORITY_QUEUE	4. PRIORITY_QUEUE	5. HEAP PRIORITY_QUEUE	6. BOUNDED_QUEU E
7. QUEUE	8. DISPENSER	9. ARRAYED_QUEUE	10. BOUNDED_STACK	11. ARRAYED_STACK	12.LINKED_QUEUE

16. iteration					
1. CURSOR_TREE _ITERATOR	2. LINEAR_ITERATOR	3. ITERATOR	4. TWO_WAY _CHAIN_ITERATOR		

17. strategies					
1. SUBSET _STRATEGY	2. SUBSET _STRATEGY_HASHABLE	3. SUBSET _STRATEGY_TREE	4. SUBSET _STRATEGY_GENERIC		

15. sort					
1. COMPARABLE _STRUCT	2. SORTED_STRUCT				

Table 10 Indexes of clusters and classes

9.2 TEST RESULTS

9.2.1 THE REFERENCE TYPES OF THE BASE TYPES

class	feature	result	no exception	precondition violation	assertion violation	other exception	possible catcall
DOUBLE_REF	item	passed	10	0	0	0	0
DOUBLE_REF	hash_code	passed	10	0	0	0	0
DOUBLE_REF	sign	passed	10	0	0	0	0
DOUBLE_REF	one	passed	10	0	0	0	0
DOUBLE_REF	zero	passed	10	0	0	0	0
DOUBLE_REF	infix "<"	passed	7	3	0	0	0
DOUBLE_REF	is_equal	passed	9	1	0	0	0
DOUBLE_REF	three_way_comparison	passed	8	2	0	0	0
DOUBLE_REF	set_item	passed	10	0	0	0	0
DOUBLE_REF	divisible	passed	9	1	0	0	0
DOUBLE_REF	exponentiable	passed	7	3	0	0	0
DOUBLE_REF	is_hashable	passed	10	0	0	0	0
DOUBLE_REF	truncated_to_integer	passed	10	0	0	0	0
DOUBLE_REF	truncated_to_integer_64	passed	10	0	0	0	0
DOUBLE_REF	truncated_to_real	passed	10	0	0	0	0
DOUBLE_REF	ceiling	passed	10	0	0	0	0
DOUBLE_REF	floor	passed	10	0	0	0	0
DOUBLE_REF	rounded	passed	10	0	0	0	0
DOUBLE_REF	abs	passed	10	0	0	0	0
DOUBLE_REF	infix "+"	passed	7	3	0	0	0
DOUBLE_REF	infix "-"	passed	10	0	0	0	0
DOUBLE_REF	infix "*"	passed	9	1	0	0	0
DOUBLE_REF	infix "/"	passed	9	1	0	0	0
DOUBLE_REF	infix "^"	passed	10	0	0	0	0
DOUBLE_REF	prefix "+"	passed	10	0	0	0	0
DOUBLE_REF	prefix "-"	passed	10	0	0	0	0
DOUBLE_REF	out	passed	10	0	0	0	0
DOUBLE_REF	generator	passed	10	0	0	0	0
DOUBLE_REF	generating_type	passed	10	0	0	0	0
DOUBLE_REF	conforms_to	passed	10	0	0	0	0
DOUBLE_REF	same_type	passed	10	0	0	0	0
DOUBLE_REF	consistent	passed	10	0	0	0	0
DOUBLE_REF	standard_is_equal	passed	7	3	0	0	0
DOUBLE_REF	equal	failed	5	0	0	0	5
DOUBLE_REF	standard_equal	failed	3	0	0	0	7
DOUBLE_REF	deep_equal	failed	3	0	0	0	7
DOUBLE_REF	copy	passed	9	1	0	0	0
DOUBLE_REF	standard_copy	passed	9	1	0	0	0
DOUBLE_REF	clone	passed	10	0	0	0	0
DOUBLE_REF	standard_clone	passed	10	0	0	0	0
DOUBLE_REF	standard_twin	passed	10	0	0	0	0
DOUBLE_REF	deep_clone	passed	10	0	0	0	0
DOUBLE_REF	deep_copy	passed	7	3	0	0	0
DOUBLE_REF	setup	passed	10	0	0	0	0
DOUBLE_REF	io	passed	10	0	0	0	0
DOUBLE_REF	tagged_out	passed	10	0	0	0	0
DOUBLE_REF	print	passed	10	0	0	0	0
DOUBLE_REF	Operating_environment	passed	10	0	0	0	0
DOUBLE_REF	default_rescue	passed	10	0	0	0	0
DOUBLE_REF	default_create	passed	10	0	0	0	0
DOUBLE_REF	do_nothing	passed	10	0	0	0	0
DOUBLE_REF	default	passed	10	0	0	0	0

DOUBLE_REF	default_pointer	passed	10	0	0	0	0
DOUBLE_REF	Void	passed	10	0	0	0	0
DOUBLE_REF	infix "<="	passed	10	0	0	0	0
DOUBLE_REF	infix ">"	passed	8	2	0	0	0
DOUBLE_REF	infix ">="	passed	9	1	0	0	0
DOUBLE_REF	max	passed	8	2	0	0	0
DOUBLE_REF	min	passed	10	0	0	0	0
REAL_REF	item	passed	10	0	0	0	0
REAL_REF	hash_code	passed	10	0	0	0	0
REAL_REF	sign	passed	10	0	0	0	0
REAL_REF	one	passed	10	0	0	0	0
REAL_REF	zero	passed	10	0	0	0	0
REAL_REF	infix "<"	passed	8	2	0	0	0
REAL_REF	is_equal	passed	8	2	0	0	0
REAL_REF	three_way_comparison	passed	9	1	0	0	0
REAL_REF	set_item	passed	10	0	0	0	0
REAL_REF	divisible	passed	8	2	0	0	0
REAL_REF	exponentiable	passed	9	1	0	0	0
REAL_REF	is_hashable	passed	10	0	0	0	0
REAL_REF	truncated_to_integer	passed	10	0	0	0	0
REAL_REF	truncated_to_integer_64	passed	10	0	0	0	0
REAL_REF	ceiling	passed	10	0	0	0	0
REAL_REF	floor	passed	10	0	0	0	0
REAL_REF	rounded	passed	10	0	0	0	0
REAL_REF	abs	passed	10	0	0	0	0
REAL_REF	infix "+"	passed	9	1	0	0	0
REAL_REF	infix "-"	passed	8	2	0	0	0
REAL_REF	infix "*"	passed	9	1	0	0	0
REAL_REF	infix "/"	passed	8	2	0	0	0
REAL_REF	infix "^"	passed	10	0	0	0	0
REAL_REF	prefix "+"	passed	10	0	0	0	0
REAL_REF	prefix "-"	passed	10	0	0	0	0
REAL_REF	out	passed	10	0	0	0	0
REAL_REF	generator	passed	10	0	0	0	0
REAL_REF	generating_type	passed	10	0	0	0	0
REAL_REF	conforms_to	passed	7	3	0	0	0
REAL_REF	same_type	passed	10	0	0	0	0
REAL_REF	consistent	passed	10	0	0	0	0
REAL_REF	standard_is_equal	passed	9	1	0	0	0
REAL_REF	equal	failed	3	0	0	0	7
REAL_REF	standard_equal	failed	3	0	0	0	7
REAL_REF	deep_equal	failed	2	0	0	0	8
REAL_REF	copy	passed	9	1	0	0	0
REAL_REF	standard_copy	passed	8	2	0	0	0
REAL_REF	clone	passed	10	0	0	0	0
REAL_REF	standard_clone	passed	10	0	0	0	0
REAL_REF	standard_twin	passed	10	0	0	0	0
REAL_REF	deep_clone	passed	10	0	0	0	0
REAL_REF	deep_copy	passed	9	1	0	0	0
REAL_REF	setup	passed	10	0	0	0	0
REAL_REF	io	passed	10	0	0	0	0
REAL_REF	tagged_out	passed	10	0	0	0	0
REAL_REF	print	passed	10	0	0	0	0
REAL_REF	Operating_environment	passed	10	0	0	0	0
REAL_REF	default_rescue	passed	10	0	0	0	0
REAL_REF	default_create	passed	10	0	0	0	0
REAL_REF	do_nothing	passed	10	0	0	0	0
REAL_REF	default	passed	10	0	0	0	0
REAL_REF	default_pointer	passed	10	0	0	0	0
REAL_REF	Void	passed	10	0	0	0	0
REAL_REF	infix "<="	passed	5	5	0	0	0
REAL_REF	infix ">"	passed	10	0	0	0	0

78

REAL_REF	infix ">="	passed	10	0	0	0	0
REAL_REF	max	passed	9	1	0	0	0
REAL_REF	min	passed	10	0	0	0	0
CHARACTER_REF	item	passed	10	0	0	0	0
CHARACTER_REF	code	passed	10	0	0	0	0
CHARACTER_REF	hash_code	passed	10	0	0	0	0
CHARACTER_REF	Min_value	passed	10	0	0	0	0
CHARACTER_REF	Max_value	passed	10	0	0	0	0
CHARACTER_REF	is_hashable	passed	10	0	0	0	0
CHARACTER_REF	infix "<"	passed	10	0	0	0	0
CHARACTER_REF	is_equal	passed	7	3	0	0	0
CHARACTER_REF	three_way_comparison	passed	9	1	0	0	0
CHARACTER_REF	infix "+"	passed	3	7	0	0	0
CHARACTER_REF	infix "-"	passed	5	5	0	0	0
CHARACTER_REF	infix "|-|"	passed	10	0	0	0	0
CHARACTER_REF	next	passed	10	0	0	0	0
CHARACTER_REF	previous	passed	10	0	0	0	0
CHARACTER_REF	set_item	passed	10	0	0	0	0
CHARACTER_REF	out	passed	10	0	0	0	0
CHARACTER_REF	as_upper	passed	10	0	0	0	0
CHARACTER_REF	upper	passed	10	0	0	0	0
CHARACTER_REF	as_lower	passed	10	0	0	0	0
CHARACTER_REF	lower	passed	10	0	0	0	0
CHARACTER_REF	is_lower	passed	10	0	0	0	0
CHARACTER_REF	is_upper	passed	10	0	0	0	0
CHARACTER_REF	is_digit	passed	10	0	0	0	0
CHARACTER_REF	is_alpha	passed	10	0	0	0	0
CHARACTER_REF	infix "<="	passed	10	0	0	0	0
CHARACTER_REF	infix ">"	passed	10	0	0	0	0
CHARACTER_REF	infix ">="	passed	9	1	0	0	0
CHARACTER_REF	max	passed	9	1	0	0	0
CHARACTER_REF	min	passed	9	1	0	0	0
CHARACTER_REF	generator	passed	10	0	0	0	0
CHARACTER_REF	generating_type	passed	10	0	0	0	0
CHARACTER_REF	conforms_to	passed	8	2	0	0	0
CHARACTER_REF	same_type	passed	10	0	0	0	0
CHARACTER_REF	consistent	passed	10	0	0	0	0
CHARACTER_REF	standard_is_equal	passed	10	0	0	0	0
CHARACTER_REF	equal	failed	1	0	0	0	9
CHARACTER_REF	standard_equal	failed	6	0	0	0	4
CHARACTER_REF	deep_equal	failed	2	0	0	0	8
CHARACTER_REF	copy	passed	9	1	0	0	0
CHARACTER_REF	standard_copy	passed	10	0	0	0	0
CHARACTER_REF	clone	passed	10	0	0	0	0
CHARACTER_REF	standard_clone	passed	10	0	0	0	0
CHARACTER_REF	standard_twin	passed	10	0	0	0	0
CHARACTER_REF	deep_clone	passed	10	0	0	0	0
CHARACTER_REF	deep_copy	passed	10	0	0	0	0
CHARACTER_REF	setup	passed	10	0	0	0	0
CHARACTER_REF	io	passed	10	0	0	0	0
CHARACTER_REF	tagged_out	passed	10	0	0	0	0
CHARACTER_REF	print	passed	10	0	0	0	0
CHARACTER_REF	Operating_environment	passed	10	0	0	0	0
CHARACTER_REF	default_rescue	passed	10	0	0	0	0
CHARACTER_REF	default_create	passed	10	0	0	0	0
CHARACTER_REF	do_nothing	passed	10	0	0	0	0
CHARACTER_REF	default	passed	10	0	0	0	0
CHARACTER_REF	default_pointer	passed	10	0	0	0	0
CHARACTER_REF	Void	passed	10	0	0	0	0
BOOLEAN_REF	item	passed	10	0	0	0	0
BOOLEAN_REF	hash_code	passed	10	0	0	0	0
BOOLEAN_REF	is_hashable	passed	10	0	0	0	0

BOOLEAN_REF	to_integer	passed	10	0	0	0	0
BOOLEAN_REF	set_item	passed	10	0	0	0	0
BOOLEAN_REF	infix "and"	passed	7	3	0	0	0
BOOLEAN_REF	infix "and then"	passed	3	7	0	0	0
BOOLEAN_REF	infix "implies"	passed	8	2	0	0	0
BOOLEAN_REF	prefix "not"	passed	10	0	0	0	0
BOOLEAN_REF	infix "or"	passed	6	4	0	0	0
BOOLEAN_REF	infix "or else"	passed	8	2	0	0	0
BOOLEAN_REF	infix "xor"	passed	8	2	0	0	0
BOOLEAN_REF	out	passed	10	0	0	0	0
BOOLEAN_REF	generator	passed	10	0	0	0	0
BOOLEAN_REF	generating_type	passed	10	0	0	0	0
BOOLEAN_REF	conforms_to	passed	10	0	0	0	0
BOOLEAN_REF	same_type	passed	10	0	0	0	0
BOOLEAN_REF	consistent	passed	10	0	0	0	0
BOOLEAN_REF	is_equal	passed	4	6	0	0	0
BOOLEAN_REF	standard_is_equal	passed	6	4	0	0	0
BOOLEAN_REF	equal	failed	0	0	0	0	10
BOOLEAN_REF	standard_equal	failed	5	0	0	0	5
BOOLEAN_REF	deep_equal	failed	6	0	0	0	4
BOOLEAN_REF	copy	passed	9	1	0	0	0
BOOLEAN_REF	standard_copy	passed	6	4	0	0	0
BOOLEAN_REF	clone	passed	10	0	0	0	0
BOOLEAN_REF	standard_clone	passed	10	0	0	0	0
BOOLEAN_REF	standard_twin	passed	10	0	0	0	0
BOOLEAN_REF	deep_clone	passed	10	0	0	0	0
BOOLEAN_REF	deep_copy	passed	5	5	0	0	0
BOOLEAN_REF	setup	passed	10	0	0	0	0
BOOLEAN_REF	io	passed	10	0	0	0	0
BOOLEAN_REF	tagged_out	passed	10	0	0	0	0
BOOLEAN_REF	print	passed	10	0	0	0	0
BOOLEAN_REF	Operating_environment	passed	10	0	0	0	0
BOOLEAN_REF	default_rescue	passed	10	0	0	0	0
BOOLEAN_REF	default_create	passed	10	0	0	0	0
BOOLEAN_REF	do_nothing	passed	10	0	0	0	0
BOOLEAN_REF	default	passed	10	0	0	0	0
BOOLEAN_REF	default_pointer	passed	10	0	0	0	0
BOOLEAN_REF	Void	passed	10	0	0	0	0
INTEGER_REF	item	passed	10	0	0	0	0
INTEGER_REF	hash_code	passed	10	0	0	0	0
INTEGER_REF	sign	passed	10	0	0	0	0
INTEGER_REF	one	passed	10	0	0	0	0
INTEGER_REF	zero	passed	10	0	0	0	0
INTEGER_REF	ascii_char	passed	6	4	0	0	0
INTEGER_REF	Min_value	passed	10	0	0	0	0
INTEGER_REF	Max_value	passed	10	0	0	0	0
INTEGER_REF	infix "<"	passed	10	0	0	0	0
INTEGER_REF	is_equal	passed	10	0	0	0	0
INTEGER_REF	three_way_comparison	passed	10	0	0	0	0
INTEGER_REF	set_item	passed	10	0	0	0	0
INTEGER_REF	divisible	passed	8	2	0	0	0
INTEGER_REF	exponentiable	passed	9	1	0	0	0
INTEGER_REF	is_hashable	passed	10	0	0	0	0
INTEGER_REF	is_valid_character_code	passed	10	0	0	0	0
INTEGER_REF	abs	passed	10	0	0	0	0
INTEGER_REF	infix "+"	passed	6	4	0	0	0
INTEGER_REF	infix "-"	passed	8	2	0	0	0
INTEGER_REF	infix "*"	passed	5	5	0	0	0
INTEGER_REF	infix "/"	passed	6	4	0	0	0
INTEGER_REF	prefix "+"	passed	10	0	0	0	0
INTEGER_REF	prefix "-"	passed	10	0	0	0	0
INTEGER_REF	infix "//"	passed	9	1	0	0	0

80

INTEGER_REF	infix "\\\\"	passed	6	4	0	0	0
INTEGER_REF	infix "^"	passed	10	0	0	0	0
INTEGER_REF	infix "|..|"	passed	10	0	0	0	0
INTEGER_REF	to_boolean	passed	10	0	0	0	0
INTEGER_REF	to_integer_8	passed	4	6	0	0	0
INTEGER_REF	to_integer_16	passed	9	1	0	0	0
INTEGER_REF	to_integer	passed	10	0	0	0	0
INTEGER_REF	to_integer_32	passed	10	0	0	0	0
INTEGER_REF	to_integer_64	passed	10	0	0	0	0
INTEGER_REF	to_hex_string	passed	10	0	0	0	0
INTEGER_REF	to_hex_character	passed	1	9	0	0	0
INTEGER_REF	to_character	passed	5	5	0	0	0
INTEGER_REF	infix "&"	passed	8	2	0	0	0
INTEGER_REF	bit_and	passed	9	1	0	0	0
INTEGER_REF	infix "|"	passed	9	1	0	0	0
INTEGER_REF	bit_or	passed	8	2	0	0	0
INTEGER_REF	bit_xor	passed	9	1	0	0	0
INTEGER_REF	bit_not	passed	10	0	0	0	0
INTEGER_REF	bit_shift	passed	6	4	0	0	0
INTEGER_REF	infix "|<<"	passed	6	4	0	0	0
INTEGER_REF	bit_shift_left	passed	3	7	0	0	0
INTEGER_REF	infix "|>>"	passed	3	7	0	0	0
INTEGER_REF	bit_shift_right	passed	1	9	0	0	0
INTEGER_REF	bit_test	passed	2	8	0	0	0
INTEGER_REF	set_bit	no call was valid	0	10	0	0	0
INTEGER_REF	set_bit_with_mask	passed	10	0	0	0	0
INTEGER_REF	out	passed	10	0	0	0	0
INTEGER_REF	generator	passed	10	0	0	0	0
INTEGER_REF	generating_type	passed	10	0	0	0	0
INTEGER_REF	conforms_to	passed	8	2	0	0	0
INTEGER_REF	same_type	passed	10	0	0	0	0
INTEGER_REF	consistent	passed	10	0	0	0	0
INTEGER_REF	standard_is_equal	passed	5	5	0	0	0
INTEGER_REF	equal	failed	3	0	0	0	7
INTEGER_REF	standard_equal	failed	2	0	0	0	8
INTEGER_REF	deep_equal	failed	4	0	0	0	6
INTEGER_REF	copy	passed	8	2	0	0	0
INTEGER_REF	standard_copy	passed	9	1	0	0	0
INTEGER_REF	clone	passed	10	0	0	0	0
INTEGER_REF	standard_clone	passed	10	0	0	0	0
INTEGER_REF	standard_twin	passed	10	0	0	0	0
INTEGER_REF	deep_clone	passed	10	0	0	0	0
INTEGER_REF	deep_copy	passed	9	1	0	0	0
INTEGER_REF	setup	passed	10	0	0	0	0
INTEGER_REF	io	passed	10	0	0	0	0
INTEGER_REF	tagged_out	passed	10	0	0	0	0
INTEGER_REF	print	passed	10	0	0	0	0
INTEGER_REF	Operating_environment	passed	10	0	0	0	0
INTEGER_REF	default_rescue	passed	10	0	0	0	0
INTEGER_REF	default_create	passed	10	0	0	0	0
INTEGER_REF	do_nothing	passed	10	0	0	0	0
INTEGER_REF	default	passed	10	0	0	0	0
INTEGER_REF	default_pointer	passed	10	0	0	0	0
INTEGER_REF	Void	passed	10	0	0	0	0
INTEGER_REF	infix "<="	passed	8	2	0	0	0
INTEGER_REF	infix ">"	passed	8	2	0	0	0
INTEGER_REF	infix ">="	passed	9	1	0	0	0
INTEGER_REF	max	passed	9	1	0	0	0
INTEGER_REF	min	passed	8	2	0	0	0
INTEGER_64_REF	item	passed	10	0	0	0	0
INTEGER_64_REF	hash_code	passed	10	0	0	0	0
INTEGER_64_REF	sign	passed	10	0	0	0	0

INTEGER_64_REF	one	passed	10	0	0	0	0
INTEGER_64_REF	zero	passed	10	0	0	0	0
INTEGER_64_REF	ascii_char	passed	4	6	0	0	0
INTEGER_64_REF	Min_value	passed	10	0	0	0	0
INTEGER_64_REF	Max_value	passed	10	0	0	0	0
INTEGER_64_REF	infix "<"	passed	10	0	0	0	0
INTEGER_64_REF	is_equal	passed	8	2	0	0	0
INTEGER_64_REF	three_way_comparison	passed	10	0	0	0	0
INTEGER_64_REF	set_item	passed	10	0	0	0	0
INTEGER_64_REF	divisible	passed	7	3	0	0	0
INTEGER_64_REF	exponentiable	passed	9	1	0	0	0
INTEGER_64_REF	is_hashable	passed	10	0	0	0	0
INTEGER_64_REF	is_valid_character_code	passed	10	0	0	0	0
INTEGER_64_REF	abs	passed	10	0	0	0	0
INTEGER_64_REF	infix "+"	passed	10	0	0	0	0
INTEGER_64_REF	infix "-"	passed	9	1	0	0	0
INTEGER_64_REF	infix "*"	passed	8	2	0	0	0
INTEGER_64_REF	infix "/"	passed	8	2	0	0	0
INTEGER_64_REF	prefix "+"	passed	10	0	0	0	0
INTEGER_64_REF	prefix "-"	passed	10	0	0	0	0
INTEGER_64_REF	infix "//"	passed	8	2	0	0	0
INTEGER_64_REF	infix "\\"	passed	8	2	0	0	0
INTEGER_64_REF	infix "^"	passed	10	0	0	0	0
INTEGER_64_REF	to_boolean	passed	10	0	0	0	0
INTEGER_64_REF	to_integer_8	passed	7	3	0	0	0
INTEGER_64_REF	to_integer_16	passed	8	2	0	0	0
INTEGER_64_REF	to_integer	passed	8	2	0	0	0
INTEGER_64_REF	to_integer_32	passed	8	2	0	0	0
INTEGER_64_REF	to_integer_64	passed	10	0	0	0	0
INTEGER_64_REF	to_hex_string	passed	10	0	0	0	0
INTEGER_64_REF	to_hex_character	passed	4	6	0	0	0
INTEGER_64_REF	to_character	passed	5	5	0	0	0
INTEGER_64_REF	infix "&"	passed	7	3	0	0	0
INTEGER_64_REF	bit_and	passed	8	2	0	0	0
INTEGER_64_REF	infix "|"	passed	9	1	0	0	0
INTEGER_64_REF	bit_or	passed	9	1	0	0	0
INTEGER_64_REF	bit_xor	passed	6	4	0	0	0
INTEGER_64_REF	bit_not	passed	10	0	0	0	0
INTEGER_64_REF	bit_shift	passed	6	4	0	0	0
INTEGER_64_REF	infix "|<<"	passed	3	7	0	0	0
INTEGER_64_REF	bit_shift_left	passed	4	6	0	0	0
INTEGER_64_REF	infix "|>>"	passed	4	6	0	0	0
INTEGER_64_REF	bit_shift_right	passed	2	8	0	0	0
INTEGER_64_REF	bit_test	passed	2	8	0	0	0
INTEGER_64_REF	set_bit	passed	3	7	0	0	0
INTEGER_64_REF	set_bit_with_mask	passed	10	0	0	0	0
INTEGER_64_REF	out	passed	10	0	0	0	0
INTEGER_64_REF	generator	passed	10	0	0	0	0
INTEGER_64_REF	generating_type	passed	10	0	0	0	0
INTEGER_64_REF	conforms_to	passed	10	0	0	0	0
INTEGER_64_REF	same_type	passed	9	1	0	0	0
INTEGER_64_REF	consistent	passed	10	0	0	0	0
INTEGER_64_REF	standard_is_equal	passed	10	0	0	0	0
INTEGER_64_REF	equal	failed	5	0	0	0	5
INTEGER_64_REF	standard_equal	failed	1	0	0	0	9
INTEGER_64_REF	deep_equal	failed	3	0	0	0	7
INTEGER_64_REF	copy	passed	9	1	0	0	0
INTEGER_64_REF	standard_copy	passed	9	1	0	0	0
INTEGER_64_REF	clone	passed	10	0	0	0	0
INTEGER_64_REF	standard_clone	passed	10	0	0	0	0
INTEGER_64_REF	standard_twin	passed	10	0	0	0	0
INTEGER_64_REF	deep_clone	passed	10	0	0	0	0

82

INTEGER_64_REF	deep_copy	passed	7	3	0	0	0
INTEGER_64_REF	setup	passed	10	0	0	0	0
INTEGER_64_REF	io	passed	10	0	0	0	0
INTEGER_64_REF	tagged_out	passed	10	0	0	0	0
INTEGER_64_REF	print	passed	10	0	0	0	0
INTEGER_64_REF	Operating_environment	passed	10	0	0	0	0
INTEGER_64_REF	default_rescue	passed	10	0	0	0	0
INTEGER_64_REF	default_create	passed	10	0	0	0	0
INTEGER_64_REF	do_nothing	passed	10	0	0	0	0
INTEGER_64_REF	default	passed	10	0	0	0	0
INTEGER_64_REF	default_pointer	passed	10	0	0	0	0
INTEGER_64_REF	Void	passed	10	0	0	0	0
INTEGER_64_REF	infix "<="	passed	10	0	0	0	0
INTEGER_64_REF	infix ">"	passed	9	1	0	0	0
INTEGER_64_REF	infix ">="	passed	8	2	0	0	0
INTEGER_64_REF	max	passed	6	4	0	0	0
INTEGER_64_REF	min	passed	9	1	0	0	0
INTEGER_16_REF	item	passed	10	0	0	0	0
INTEGER_16_REF	hash_code	failed	8	0	2	0	0
INTEGER_16_REF	sign	failed	9	0	1	0	0
INTEGER_16_REF	one	failed	9	0	1	0	0
INTEGER_16_REF	zero	failed	9	0	1	0	0
INTEGER_16_REF	ascii_char	failed	5	4	1	0	0
INTEGER_16_REF	Min_value	passed	10	0	0	0	0
INTEGER_16_REF	Max_value	passed	10	0	0	0	0
INTEGER_16_REF	infix "<"	passed	5	5	0	0	0
INTEGER_16_REF	is_equal	failed	5	1	4	0	0
INTEGER_16_REF	three_way_comparison	failed	6	1	3	0	0
INTEGER_16_REF	set_item	failed	6	0	4	0	0
INTEGER_16_REF	divisible	failed	5	0	5	0	0
INTEGER_16_REF	exponentiable	failed	5	2	3	0	0
INTEGER_16_REF	is_hashable	failed	7	0	3	0	0
INTEGER_16_REF	is_valid_character_code	failed	7	0	3	0	0
INTEGER_16_REF	abs	failed	5	0	5	0	0
INTEGER_16_REF	infix "+"	failed	7	1	2	0	0
INTEGER_16_REF	infix "-"	failed	4	2	4	0	0
INTEGER_16_REF	infix "*"	failed	3	2	5	0	0
INTEGER_16_REF	infix "/"	failed	2	6	2	0	0
INTEGER_16_REF	prefix "+"	failed	7	0	3	0	0
INTEGER_16_REF	prefix "-"	failed	7	0	3	0	0
INTEGER_16_REF	infix "//"	failed	1	3	6	0	0
INTEGER_16_REF	infix "\\"	failed	0	2	8	0	0
INTEGER_16_REF	infix "^"	failed	8	0	2	0	0
INTEGER_16_REF	infix "|..|"	failed	6	0	4	0	0
INTEGER_16_REF	to_boolean	failed	9	0	1	0	0
INTEGER_16_REF	to_integer_8	failed	1	6	3	0	0
INTEGER_16_REF	to_integer	failed	9	0	1	0	0
INTEGER_16_REF	to_integer_32	failed	8	0	2	0	0
INTEGER_16_REF	to_integer_16	passed	10	0	0	0	0
INTEGER_16_REF	to_integer_64	passed	10	0	0	0	0
INTEGER_16_REF	to_hex_string	failed	7	0	3	0	0
INTEGER_16_REF	to_hex_character	failed	2	3	5	0	0
INTEGER_16_REF	to_character	failed	5	3	2	0	0
INTEGER_16_REF	infix "&"	failed	4	2	4	0	0
INTEGER_16_REF	bit_and	failed	4	1	5	0	0
INTEGER_16_REF	infix "|"	failed	3	1	6	0	0
INTEGER_16_REF	bit_or	failed	2	1	7	0	0
INTEGER_16_REF	bit_xor	failed	4	2	4	0	0
INTEGER_16_REF	bit_not	failed	3	0	7	0	0
INTEGER_16_REF	bit_shift	failed	4	4	2	0	0
INTEGER_16_REF	infix "|<<"	failed	0	7	3	0	0
INTEGER_16_REF	bit_shift_left	failed	2	7	1	0	0

INTEGER_16_REF	infix "|>>"	failed	3	4	3	0	0
INTEGER_16_REF	bit_shift_right	failed	1	4	5	0	0
INTEGER_16_REF	bit_test	failed	3	5	2	0	0
INTEGER_16_REF	set_bit	failed	0	9	1	0	0
INTEGER_16_REF	set_bit_with_mask	failed	7	0	3	0	0
INTEGER_16_REF	out	failed	6	0	4	0	0
INTEGER_16_REF	generator	failed	6	0	4	0	0
INTEGER_16_REF	generating_type	failed	6	0	4	0	0
INTEGER_16_REF	conforms_to	failed	8	0	2	0	0
INTEGER_16_REF	same_type	failed	7	0	3	0	0
INTEGER_16_REF	consistent	failed	8	0	2	0	0
INTEGER_16_REF	standard_is_equal	failed	4	2	4	0	0
INTEGER_16_REF	equal	failed	2	0	0	0	8
INTEGER_16_REF	standard_equal	failed	3	0	2	0	5
INTEGER_16_REF	deep_equal	failed	2	0	1	0	7
INTEGER_16_REF	copy	failed	2	1	7	0	0
INTEGER_16_REF	standard_copy	failed	3	1	6	0	0
INTEGER_16_REF	clone	failed	7	0	3	0	0
INTEGER_16_REF	standard_clone	failed	7	0	3	0	0
INTEGER_16_REF	standard_twin	failed	7	0	3	0	0
INTEGER_16_REF	deep_clone	failed	4	0	6	0	0
INTEGER_16_REF	deep_copy	failed	3	0	7	0	0
INTEGER_16_REF	setup	failed	3	0	7	0	0
INTEGER_16_REF	io	passed	10	0	0	0	0
INTEGER_16_REF	tagged_out	failed	7	0	3	0	0
INTEGER_16_REF	print	failed	5	0	5	0	0
INTEGER_16_REF	Operating_environment	passed	10	0	0	0	0
INTEGER_16_REF	default_rescue	failed	7	0	3	0	0
INTEGER_16_REF	default_create	failed	5	0	5	0	0
INTEGER_16_REF	do_nothing	failed	6	0	4	0	0
INTEGER_16_REF	default	failed	5	0	5	0	0
INTEGER_16_REF	default_pointer	failed	7	0	3	0	0
INTEGER_16_REF	Void	passed	10	0	0	0	0
INTEGER_16_REF	infix "<="	failed	5	1	4	0	0
INTEGER_16_REF	infix ">"	failed	5	0	5	0	0
INTEGER_16_REF	infix ">="	failed	3	1	6	0	0
INTEGER_16_REF	max	failed	6	2	2	0	0
INTEGER_16_REF	min	failed	5	1	4	0	0
INTEGER_8_REF	item	passed	10	0	0	0	0
INTEGER_8_REF	hash_code	failed	7	0	3	0	0
INTEGER_8_REF	sign	failed	9	0	1	0	0
INTEGER_8_REF	one	failed	8	0	2	0	0
INTEGER_8_REF	zero	failed	8	0	2	0	0
INTEGER_8_REF	ascii_char	failed	5	1	4	0	0
INTEGER_8_REF	Min_value	passed	10	0	0	0	0
INTEGER_8_REF	Max_value	passed	10	0	0	0	0
INTEGER_8_REF	infix "<"	failed	5	2	3	0	0
INTEGER_8_REF	is_equal	failed	6	0	4	0	0
INTEGER_8_REF	three_way_comparison	passed	10	0	0	0	0
INTEGER_8_REF	set_item	failed	7	0	3	0	0
INTEGER_8_REF	divisible	failed	5	2	3	0	0
INTEGER_8_REF	exponentiable	failed	5	1	4	0	0
INTEGER_8_REF	is_hashable	failed	8	0	2	0	0
INTEGER_8_REF	is_valid_character_code	failed	7	0	3	0	0
INTEGER_8_REF	abs	failed	7	0	3	0	0
INTEGER_8_REF	infix "+"	failed	3	0	7	0	0
INTEGER_8_REF	infix "-"	failed	3	2	5	0	0
INTEGER_8_REF	infix "*"	failed	2	1	7	0	0
INTEGER_8_REF	infix "/"	failed	3	0	7	0	0
INTEGER_8_REF	prefix "+"	failed	6	0	4	0	0
INTEGER_8_REF	prefix "-"	passed	10	0	0	0	0
INTEGER_8_REF	infix "//"	failed	5	1	4	0	0

INTEGER_8_REF	infix "\\"	failed	4	1	5	0	0
INTEGER_8_REF	infix "^"	failed	6	0	4	0	0
INTEGER_8_REF	infix "|..|"	failed	5	0	5	0	0
INTEGER_8_REF	to_boolean	failed	7	0	3	0	0
INTEGER_8_REF	to_integer_8	failed	7	0	3	0	0
INTEGER_8_REF	to_integer_16	failed	5	0	5	0	0
INTEGER_8_REF	to_integer	failed	6	0	4	0	0
INTEGER_8_REF	to_integer_32	failed	8	0	2	0	0
INTEGER_8_REF	to_integer_64	failed	6	0	4	0	0
INTEGER_8_REF	to_hex_string	failed	7	0	3	0	0
INTEGER_8_REF	to_hex_character	failed	7	1	2	0	0
INTEGER_8_REF	to_character	failed	6	3	1	0	0
INTEGER_8_REF	infix "&"	failed	4	1	5	0	0
INTEGER_8_REF	bit_and	failed	4	1	5	0	0
INTEGER_8_REF	infix "|"	failed	6	0	4	0	0
INTEGER_8_REF	bit_or	failed	8	0	2	0	0
INTEGER_8_REF	bit_xor	failed	3	0	7	0	0
INTEGER_8_REF	bit_not	failed	7	0	3	0	0
INTEGER_8_REF	bit_shift	failed	1	6	3	0	0
INTEGER_8_REF	infix "|<<"	failed	2	7	1	0	0
INTEGER_8_REF	bit_shift_left	failed	1	7	2	0	0
INTEGER_8_REF	infix "|>>"	failed	2	3	5	0	0
INTEGER_8_REF	bit_shift_right	failed	2	4	4	0	0
INTEGER_8_REF	bit_test	failed	0	8	2	0	0
INTEGER_8_REF	set_bit	failed	0	3	7	0	0
INTEGER_8_REF	set_bit_with_mask	failed	6	0	4	0	0
INTEGER_8_REF	out	failed	9	0	1	0	0
INTEGER_8_REF	generator	failed	3	0	7	0	0
INTEGER_8_REF	generating_type	failed	7	0	3	0	0
INTEGER_8_REF	conforms_to	failed	9	0	1	0	0
INTEGER_8_REF	same_type	failed	6	0	4	0	0
INTEGER_8_REF	consistent	failed	3	0	7	0	0
INTEGER_8_REF	standard_is_equal	failed	4	0	6	0	0
INTEGER_8_REF	equal	failed	1	0	3	0	6
INTEGER_8_REF	standard_equal	failed	5	0	1	0	4
INTEGER_8_REF	deep_equal	failed	3	0	3	0	4
INTEGER_8_REF	copy	failed	4	2	4	0	0
INTEGER_8_REF	standard_copy	failed	5	1	4	0	0
INTEGER_8_REF	clone	failed	8	0	2	0	0
INTEGER_8_REF	standard_clone	failed	5	0	5	0	0
INTEGER_8_REF	standard_twin	failed	5	0	5	0	0
INTEGER_8_REF	deep_clone	failed	5	0	5	0	0
INTEGER_8_REF	deep_copy	failed	3	2	5	0	0
INTEGER_8_REF	setup	failed	5	0	5	0	0
INTEGER_8_REF	io	passed	10	0	0	0	0
INTEGER_8_REF	tagged_out	failed	7	0	3	0	0
INTEGER_8_REF	print	failed	7	0	3	0	0
INTEGER_8_REF	Operating_environment	passed	10	0	0	0	0
INTEGER_8_REF	default_rescue	failed	7	0	3	0	0
INTEGER_8_REF	default_create	failed	5	0	5	0	0
INTEGER_8_REF	do_nothing	failed	6	0	4	0	0
INTEGER_8_REF	default	failed	5	0	5	0	0
INTEGER_8_REF	default_pointer	failed	7	0	3	0	0
INTEGER_8_REF	Void	passed	10	0	0	0	0
INTEGER_8_REF	infix "<="	failed	5	1	4	0	0
INTEGER_8_REF	infix ">"	failed	4	1	5	0	0
INTEGER_8_REF	infix ">="	failed	3	3	4	0	0
INTEGER_8_REF	max	failed	4	2	4	0	0
INTEGER_8_REF	min	failed	5	0	5	0	0

9.2.2 CLUSTER KERNEL_CLASSIC

class	feature	result	no exception	precondition violation	assertion violation	other exception	possible catcall
ANY	generator	passed	10	0	0	0	0
ANY	generating_type	passed	10	0	0	0	0
ANY	conforms_to	passed	10	0	0	0	0
ANY	same_type	passed	10	0	0	0	0
ANY	consistent	failed	2	0	0	0	8
ANY	is_equal	failed	0	2	0	0	8
ANY	standard_is_equal	failed	1	0	0	0	9
ANY	equal	failed	2	0	0	0	8
ANY	standard_equal	failed	0	0	0	0	10
ANY	deep_equal	failed	2	0	0	0	8
ANY	copy	failed	0	3	0	0	7
ANY	standard_copy	failed	1	0	0	0	9
ANY	clone	passed	10	0	0	0	0
ANY	standard_clone	passed	10	0	0	0	0
ANY	standard_twin	passed	10	0	0	0	0
ANY	deep_clone	passed	10	0	0	0	0
ANY	deep_copy	failed	1	1	0	0	8
ANY	setup	failed	3	0	0	0	7
ANY	io	passed	10	0	0	0	0
ANY	out	passed	10	0	0	0	0
ANY	tagged_out	passed	10	0	0	0	0
ANY	print	passed	10	0	0	0	0
ANY	Operating_environment	passed	10	0	0	0	0
ANY	default_rescue	passed	10	0	0	0	0
ANY	default_create	passed	10	0	0	0	0
ANY	do_nothing	passed	10	0	0	0	0
ANY	default	passed	10	0	0	0	0
ANY	default_pointer	passed	10	0	0	0	0
ANY	Void	passed	10	0	0	0	0
TUPLE	make	passed	10	0	0	0	0
TUPLE	item	no call was valid	0	10	0	0	0
TUPLE	infix "@"	no call was valid	0	10	0	0	0
TUPLE	reference_item	no call was valid	0	10	0	0	0
TUPLE	boolean_item	no call was valid	0	10	0	0	0
TUPLE	character_item	no call was valid	0	10	0	0	0
TUPLE	double_item	no call was valid	0	10	0	0	0
TUPLE	integer_8_item	no call was valid	0	10	0	0	0
TUPLE	integer_16_item	no call was valid	0	10	0	0	0
TUPLE	integer_item	no call was valid	0	10	0	0	0
TUPLE	integer_32_item	no call was valid	0	10	0	0	0
TUPLE	integer_64_item	no call was valid	0	10	0	0	0
TUPLE	pointer_item	no call was valid	0	10	0	0	0
TUPLE	real_item	no call was valid	0	10	0	0	0
TUPLE	hash_code	passed	10	0	0	0	0
TUPLE	valid_index	passed	10	0	0	0	0
TUPLE	valid_type_for_index	no call was valid	0	10	0	0	0
TUPLE	count	passed	10	0	0	0	0
TUPLE	lower	passed	10	0	0	0	0
TUPLE	upper	passed	10	0	0	0	0
TUPLE	is_empty	passed	10	0	0	0	0
TUPLE	put	no call was valid	0	10	0	0	0
TUPLE	put_reference	no call was valid	0	10	0	0	0
TUPLE	put_boolean	no call was valid	0	10	0	0	0
TUPLE	put_character	no call was valid	0	10	0	0	0
TUPLE	put_double	no call was valid	0	10	0	0	0
TUPLE	put_real	no call was valid	0	10	0	0	0
TUPLE	put_pointer	no call was valid	0	10	0	0	0

TUPLE	put_integer	no call was valid	0	10	0	0	0
TUPLE	put_integer_32	no call was valid	0	10	0	0	0
TUPLE	put_integer_8	no call was valid	0	10	0	0	0
TUPLE	put_integer_16	no call was valid	0	10	0	0	0
TUPLE	put_integer_64	no call was valid	0	10	0	0	0
TUPLE	is_boolean_item	no call was valid	0	10	0	0	0
TUPLE	is_character_item	no call was valid	0	10	0	0	0
TUPLE	is_wide_character_item	no call was valid	0	10	0	0	0
TUPLE	is_double_item	no call was valid	0	10	0	0	0
TUPLE	is_integer_8_item	no call was valid	0	10	0	0	0
TUPLE	is_integer_16_item	no call was valid	0	10	0	0	0
TUPLE	is_integer_item	no call was valid	0	10	0	0	0
TUPLE	is_integer_32_item	no call was valid	0	10	0	0	0
TUPLE	is_integer_64_item	no call was valid	0	10	0	0	0
TUPLE	is_pointer_item	no call was valid	0	10	0	0	0
TUPLE	is_real_item	no call was valid	0	10	0	0	0
TUPLE	is_reference_item	no call was valid	0	10	0	0	0
TUPLE	is_numeric_item	no call was valid	0	10	0	0	0
TUPLE	is_uniform	passed	10	0	0	0	0
TUPLE	is_uniform_boolean	passed	10	0	0	0	0
TUPLE	is_uniform_character	passed	10	0	0	0	0
TUPLE	is_uniform_wide_character	passed	10	0	0	0	0
TUPLE	is_uniform_double	passed	10	0	0	0	0
TUPLE	is_uniform_integer_8	passed	10	0	0	0	0
TUPLE	is_uniform_integer_16	passed	10	0	0	0	0
TUPLE	is_uniform_integer	passed	10	0	0	0	0
TUPLE	is_uniform_integer_32	passed	10	0	0	0	0
TUPLE	is_uniform_integer_64	passed	10	0	0	0	0
TUPLE	is_uniform_pointer	passed	10	0	0	0	0
TUPLE	is_uniform_real	passed	10	0	0	0	0
TUPLE	is_uniform_reference	passed	10	0	0	0	0
TUPLE	convertible_to_double	passed	10	0	0	0	0
TUPLE	convertible_to_real	passed	10	0	0	0	0
TUPLE	arrayed	passed	10	0	0	0	0
TUPLE	boolean_arrayed	passed	10	0	0	0	0
TUPLE	character_arrayed	passed	10	0	0	0	0
TUPLE	double_arrayed	passed	10	0	0	0	0
TUPLE	integer_arrayed	passed	10	0	0	0	0
TUPLE	pointer_arrayed	passed	10	0	0	0	0
TUPLE	real_arrayed	passed	10	0	0	0	0
TUPLE	string_arrayed	passed	10	0	0	0	0
TUPLE	correct_mismatch	failed	0	0	0	10	0
TUPLE	is_hashable	passed	10	0	0	0	0
TUPLE	generator	passed	10	0	0	0	0
TUPLE	generating_type	passed	10	0	0	0	0
TUPLE	conforms_to	passed	10	0	0	0	0
TUPLE	same_type	passed	10	0	0	0	0
TUPLE	consistent	passed	10	0	0	0	0
TUPLE	is_equal	passed	3	7	0	0	0
TUPLE	standard_is_equal	passed	5	5	0	0	0
TUPLE	equal	failed	2	0	0	0	8
TUPLE	standard_equal	failed	3	0	0	0	7
TUPLE	deep_equal	failed	1	0	0	0	9
TUPLE	copy	passed	6	4	0	0	0
TUPLE	standard_copy	passed	5	5	0	0	0
TUPLE	clone	passed	10	0	0	0	0
TUPLE	standard_clone	passed	10	0	0	0	0
TUPLE	standard_twin	passed	10	0	0	0	0
TUPLE	deep_clone	passed	10	0	0	0	0
TUPLE	deep_copy	passed	2	8	0	0	0
TUPLE	setup	passed	10	0	0	0	0
TUPLE	io	passed	10	0	0	0	0

TUPLE	out	passed	10	0	0	0	0
TUPLE	tagged_out	passed	10	0	0	0	0
TUPLE	print	passed	10	0	0	0	0
TUPLE	Operating_environment	passed	10	0	0	0	0
TUPLE	default_rescue	passed	10	0	0	0	0
TUPLE	default_create	passed	10	0	0	0	0
TUPLE	do_nothing	passed	10	0	0	0	0
TUPLE	default	passed	10	0	0	0	0
TUPLE	default_pointer	passed	10	0	0	0	0
TUPLE	Void	passed	10	0	0	0	0
TUPLE	mismatch_information	passed	10	0	0	0	0
STRING	make	passed	8	2	0	0	0
STRING	make_empty	passed	10	0	0	0	0
STRING	make_filled	passed	9	1	0	0	0
STRING	make_from_string	passed	8	2	0	0	0
STRING	make_from_c	no call was valid	0	10	0	0	0
STRING	from_c	no call was valid	0	10	0	0	0
STRING	from_c_substring	no call was valid	0	10	0	0	0
STRING	adapt	passed	10	0	0	0	0
STRING	remake	passed	5	5	0	0	0
STRING	item	passed	2	8	0	0	0
STRING	infix "@"	passed	2	8	0	0	0
STRING	item_code	passed	2	8	0	0	0
STRING	hash_code	passed	10	0	0	0	0
STRING	False_constant	passed	10	0	0	0	0
STRING	True_constant	passed	10	0	0	0	0
STRING	shared_with	passed	10	0	0	0	0
STRING	index_of	passed	5	5	0	0	0
STRING	last_index_of	passed	5	5	0	0	0
STRING	substring_index_in_bounds	no call was valid	0	10	0	0	0
STRING	string	passed	10	0	0	0	0
STRING	substring_index	passed	4	6	0	0	0
STRING	fuzzy_index	passed	1	9	0	0	0
STRING	capacity	passed	10	0	0	0	0
STRING	count	passed	10	0	0	0	0
STRING	occurrences	passed	10	0	0	0	0
STRING	index_set	passed	10	0	0	0	0
STRING	is_equal	passed	10	0	0	0	0
STRING	same_string	passed	9	1	0	0	0
STRING	infix "<"	passed	9	1	0	0	0
STRING	has	passed	10	0	0	0	0
STRING	has_substring	passed	7	3	0	0	0
STRING	extendible	passed	10	0	0	0	0
STRING	prunable	passed	10	0	0	0	0
STRING	valid_index	passed	10	0	0	0	0
STRING	changeable_comparison_criterion	passed	10	0	0	0	0
STRING	is_integer	passed	10	0	0	0	0
STRING	is_real	passed	10	0	0	0	0
STRING	is_double	passed	10	0	0	0	0
STRING	is_boolean	passed	10	0	0	0	0
STRING	set	passed	7	3	0	0	0
STRING	copy	passed	9	1	0	0	0
STRING	subcopy	no call was valid	0	10	0	0	0
STRING	replace_substring	passed	1	9	0	0	0
STRING	replace_substring_all	passed	3	7	0	0	0
STRING	replace_blank	passed	10	0	0	0	0
STRING	fill_blank	passed	10	0	0	0	0
STRING	fill_with	passed	10	0	0	0	0
STRING	replace_character	passed	10	0	0	0	0
STRING	fill_character	passed	10	0	0	0	0
STRING	head	passed	4	6	0	0	0
STRING	keep_head	passed	8	2	0	0	0

88

STRING	tail	passed	8	2	0	0	0
STRING	keep_tail	passed	6	4	0	0	0
STRING	left_adjust	passed	10	0	0	0	0
STRING	right_adjust	passed	10	0	0	0	0
STRING	share	passed	9	1	0	0	0
STRING	put	passed	6	4	0	0	0
STRING	precede	passed	10	0	0	0	0
STRING	prepend_character	passed	10	0	0	0	0
STRING	prepend	failed	8	1	1	0	0
STRING	prepend_boolean	passed	10	0	0	0	0
STRING	prepend_double	passed	10	0	0	0	0
STRING	prepend_integer	passed	10	0	0	0	0
STRING	prepend_real	passed	10	0	0	0	0
STRING	prepend_string	failed	6	0	4	0	0
STRING	append	passed	8	2	0	0	0
STRING	infix "+"	passed	9	1	0	0	0
STRING	append_string	passed	10	0	0	0	0
STRING	append_integer	passed	10	0	0	0	0
STRING	append_real	passed	10	0	0	0	0
STRING	append_double	passed	10	0	0	0	0
STRING	append_character	passed	10	0	0	0	0
STRING	extend	passed	10	0	0	0	0
STRING	append_boolean	passed	10	0	0	0	0
STRING	insert	passed	6	4	0	0	0
STRING	insert_string	failed	3	4	3	0	0
STRING	insert_character	passed	8	2	0	0	0
STRING	remove	passed	6	4	0	0	0
STRING	remove_head	passed	8	2	0	0	0
STRING	remove_substring	passed	1	9	0	0	0
STRING	remove_tail	passed	8	2	0	0	0
STRING	prune	passed	10	0	0	0	0
STRING	prune_all	passed	10	0	0	0	0
STRING	prune_all_leading	passed	10	0	0	0	0
STRING	prune_all_trailing	passed	10	0	0	0	0
STRING	wipe_out	passed	10	0	0	0	0
STRING	clear_all	passed	10	0	0	0	0
STRING	adapt_size	passed	10	0	0	0	0
STRING	resize	passed	8	2	0	0	0
STRING	grow	passed	10	0	0	0	0
STRING	as_lower	passed	10	0	0	0	0
STRING	as_upper	passed	10	0	0	0	0
STRING	left_justify	passed	10	0	0	0	0
STRING	center_justify	could not be tested	0	0	0	0	0
STRING	right_justify	passed	10	0	0	0	0
STRING	character_justify	could not be tested	0	0	0	0	0
STRING	to_lower	passed	10	0	0	0	0
STRING	to_upper	passed	10	0	0	0	0
STRING	to_integer	no call was valid	0	10	0	0	0
STRING	to_integer_64	no call was valid	0	10	0	0	0
STRING	to_real	no call was valid	0	10	0	0	0
STRING	to_double	no call was valid	0	10	0	0	0
STRING	to_boolean	no call was valid	0	10	0	0	0
STRING	linear_representation	passed	10	0	0	0	0
STRING	split	passed	10	0	0	0	0
STRING	to_c	passed	10	0	0	0	0
STRING	mirrored	passed	10	0	0	0	0
STRING	mirror	passed	10	0	0	0	0
STRING	substring	passed	10	0	0	0	0
STRING	multiply	passed	7	3	0	0	0
STRING	out	passed	10	0	0	0	0
STRING	is_inserted	passed	10	0	0	0	0
STRING	fill	passed	10	0	0	0	0

STRING	is_empty	passed	10	0	0	0	0
STRING	empty	passed	10	0	0	0	0
STRING	object_comparison	passed	10	0	0	0	0
STRING	compare_objects	no call was valid	0	10	0	0	0
STRING	compare_references	no call was valid	0	10	0	0	0
STRING	generator	passed	10	0	0	0	0
STRING	generating_type	passed	10	0	0	0	0
STRING	conforms_to	passed	10	0	0	0	0
STRING	same_type	passed	10	0	0	0	0
STRING	consistent	passed	10	0	0	0	0
STRING	standard_is_equal	passed	6	4	0	0	0
STRING	equal	failed	2	0	0	0	8
STRING	standard_equal	failed	1	0	0	0	9
STRING	deep_equal	failed	2	0	0	0	8
STRING	standard_copy	passed	6	4	0	0	0
STRING	clone	passed	10	0	0	0	0
STRING	standard_clone	passed	10	0	0	0	0
STRING	standard_twin	passed	10	0	0	0	0
STRING	deep_clone	passed	10	0	0	0	0
STRING	deep_copy	failed	5	2	3	0	0
STRING	setup	passed	10	0	0	0	0
STRING	io	passed	10	0	0	0	0
STRING	tagged_out	passed	10	0	0	0	0
STRING	print	passed	10	0	0	0	0
STRING	Operating_environment	passed	10	0	0	0	0
STRING	default_rescue	passed	10	0	0	0	0
STRING	default_create	passed	10	0	0	0	0
STRING	do_nothing	passed	10	0	0	0	0
STRING	default	passed	10	0	0	0	0
STRING	default_pointer	passed	10	0	0	0	0
STRING	Void	passed	10	0	0	0	0
STRING	Growth_percentage	passed	10	0	0	0	0
STRING	Minimal_increase	passed	10	0	0	0	0
STRING	additional_space	passed	10	0	0	0	0
STRING	resizable	passed	10	0	0	0	0
STRING	automatic_grow	passed	10	0	0	0	0
STRING	full	passed	10	0	0	0	0
STRING	is_hashable	passed	10	0	0	0	0
STRING	infix "<="	passed	9	1	0	0	0
STRING	infix ">"	passed	10	0	0	0	0
STRING	infix ">="	passed	9	1	0	0	0
STRING	three_way_comparison	passed	7	3	0	0	0
STRING	max	passed	8	2	0	0	0
STRING	min	passed	9	1	0	0	0
STRING	area	passed	10	0	0	0	0
STRING	mismatch_information	passed	10	0	0	0	0

10 REFERENCES

[1]   Karine Arnout, Xavier Rousselot, Bertrand Meyer: *Test Wizard: Automatic test case generation based on Design by Contract^{TM}*, draft report, ETH, June 2003. Retrieved July 2003 from
http://se.inf.ethz.ch/people/arnout_rousselot_meyer_test_wizard.pdf

[2]   Éric Bezault: *Gobo Eiffel Project*. Retrieved June 2003 from
http://www.gobosoft.com/eiffel/gobo/index.html

[3]   Éric Bezault: *Gobo Eiffel Lint*. Retrieved June 2003 from
http://cvs.sourceforge.net/cgibin/viewcvs.cgi/gobo-eiffel/gobo/src/gelint/

[4]   Éric Bezault: *Gobo Eiffel Test*. Retrieved June 2003 from
http://www.gobosoft.com/eiffel/gobo/getest/index.html

[5]   Robert V. Binder: *Testing Object-Oriented Systems, Models, Patterns, and Tools.* Addison Wesley, 1999.

[6]   Bertrand. Meyer: *Applying 'Design by Contract'*, Technical Report TR-EI-12/CO, Interactive Software Engineering Inc., 1986. Published in *IEEE Computer*, vol. 25, no. 10, October 1992, p 40-51.

[7]   Bertrand Meyer: *Eiffel: The Language*. Prentice Hall, 1992.

[8]   Bertrand Meyer: *Reusable Software: The Base Object-Oriented Component Libraries.* Prentice Hall, 1994.

[9]   Bertrand Meyer: *Object-Oriented Software Construction, 2nd edition*. Prentice Hall, 1997.

[10]   Bertrand Meyer: *Design by Contract*. Prentice Hall (in preparation).

[11]   Robert Mitchell and Jim McKim: *Design by Contract, by example.* Addison-Wesley, 2002.

[12]   Eiffel Software Inc. *EiffelBase*. Retrieved June 2003 from
http://docs.eiffel.com/libraries/base/index.html

[13]   National Institute of Standards and Technology (NIST). "The Economic Impacts of Inadequate Infrastructure for Software Testing". Planning Report 02-3 , RTI Project Number 7007.011, May 2002.
http://www.nist.gov/director/prog-ofc/report02-3.pdf

www.ingramcontent.com/pod-product-compliance
Lightning Source LLC
La Vergne TN
LVHW080101070326
832902LV00014B/2360